FIRST
FACTS
ABOUT

AMERICAN
HEROES

Dedication
For Sharon—and the love of exploration in history, literature, and the world around us.

ISBN 0-439-13583-4

12 11 10 9 8 7 6 5 4 3 2 1   9/9 0 1 2 3 4/0

Printed in the U.S.A.   14

First Scholastic Printing, October 1999

FIRST
FACTS
ABOUT

AMERICAN
HEROES

★ ★ ★

by

David C. King

SCHOLASTIC INC.

New York Toronto London Auckland Sydney
Mexico City New Delhi Hong Kong

Contents

★ 1

Colonial America

Between 1607 and 1730, thousands of European settlers braved a dangerous ocean crossing in flimsy sailing ships. They came to a "New World" that was a wilderness to them; it was an untamed land that claimed the lives of many. Of course, this so-called New World was not new to all the people of the Native-American tribes that had lived here for many centuries. Survival was second nature to the Indians, and they helped the first settlers at Jamestown (Virginia) and Plymouth (Massachusetts) get through the hardest years of settlement. Perhaps the first true American heroes included both settlers and the Indians who helped them.

Thirteen colonies ruled by Great Britain gradually took hold and grew prosperous. The Native Americans realized too late that the newcomers were taking over their lands and threatening their way of life. Some of the tribes fought back. Others moved west beyond the Appalachian Mountains, not realizing that land-hungry settlers would soon follow. In 1754, many of the tribes joined with the French in Canada in a war to defeat the British colonies. In this French and Indian War, though, the British, with help from the colonists, drove the French out of North America.

Britain's colonies continued to grow. But some people came to America against their will—they were brought from Africa as slaves. The first Africans arrived at Jamestown Colony as servants in 1619. Soon Africans were being sold as slaves in all thirteen colonies. In the South, where colonists developed huge plantations, there were many more slaves. While some African Americans gained their freedom, the great majority would live in bondage until the Civil War (1861-1865), the "War Between the States" that was fought between the North and South over the slavery issue. Even before the war, some African Americans would emerge as heroes to their people and to the nation.

A Native American greets the Plymouth settlers.

C H R O N O L O G Y

1607 Captain John Smith and a band of British men and boys arrive at Jamestown

1614 Squanto and John Smith map the coastline of New England

1615 Squanto is sold into slavery

1619 The first African indentured servants arrive at Jamestown

1620 The Mayflower lands off Plymouth

1621 The first Thanksgiving is celebrated

1634 Anne Hutchinson arrives in New England

1637 Anne Hutchinson is put on trial and banished from the Massachusetts Bay Colony

1643 Anne Hutchinson is killed in an Indian raid

1644 The colony of Rhode Island is recognized by England

1681 Charles II of England grants William Penn's father a large tract of land in America

1682–1684 William Penn establishes a colony in Pennsylvania

1754–1763 The French and Indian War is fought

1755 Daniel Boone escapes from his captors during the French and Indian War

1776 Jemima Boone is kidnapped by Native-American warriors

1778 Daniel Boone is captured by the Shawnees

JOHN SMITH

EXPLORER, COLONIAL LEADER, SOLDIER, AND WRITER

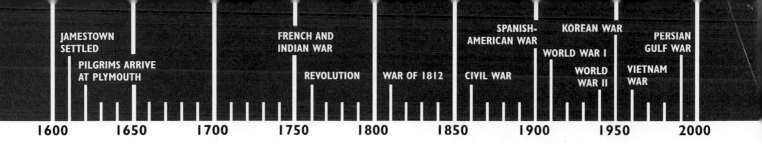

| JAMESTOWN SETTLED | | FRENCH AND INDIAN WAR | | | SPANISH-AMERICAN WAR | KOREAN WAR | PERSIAN GULF WAR |
| PILGRIMS ARRIVE AT PLYMOUTH | | | REVOLUTION | WAR OF 1812 | CIVIL WAR | WORLD WAR I / WORLD WAR II | VIETNAM WAR |

1600   1650   1700   1750   1800   1850   1900   1950   2000

- Born about 1580, in Willoughby, England
- Helped establish the first permanent English colony in America
- Explored and named New England
- Died in June 1631, in London, England

In 1607, a band of British men and boys struggled ashore on the coast of Virginia. A total of 144 had left England, but only 45 would survive the ocean voyage to America and the first winter there. Captain John Smith was one of those survivors. Thanks to his leadership, Jamestown survived to become the first permanent English settlement in America.

For several years, Smith's strong leadership saved the colonists from starvation. The men were only

Pocahontas pleads for John Smith's life.

interested in searching for gold. Smith forced them to work—to build homes and plant vegetables, such as Indian corn. He also explored much of what is now Virginia. You may know the most famous story about John Smith: He was captured by Indians and was sentenced to death by their chief, Powhatan. But at the last second, Powhatan's 12-year-old daughter, Pocahontas, persuaded the chief to spare him.

Injuries suffered in a gunpowder explosion forced Smith to return to England. Five years later, he came back to North America and explored the coast of the region that he named New England. His books and maps helped the first settlers there: the Pilgrims.

The first day at Jamestown.

PRISON EXPERIENCES
John Smith's capture by Powhatan's men was not the only time that he found himself a prisoner. In 1600, while fighting a war in Europe, he was taken prisoner and made a slave by Turks. And in 1615, after his adventures in America, he was seized by pirates and held prisoner for several months.

A STARVING TIME
After Smith left Jamestown, the colony was badly managed and suffered through the "starving time" of 1609-1610. Of the 800 settlers, only 60 survived, by eating corn stalks and rats.

UPDATE
John Smith's adventures were so amazing that many people refused to believe that the stories he wrote, including his rescue by Pocahontas, were based on fact. In the 1960s, however, historians concluded that most of his stories really happened.

9

SQUANTO

FRIEND OF THE PILGRIMS AND EXPLORER

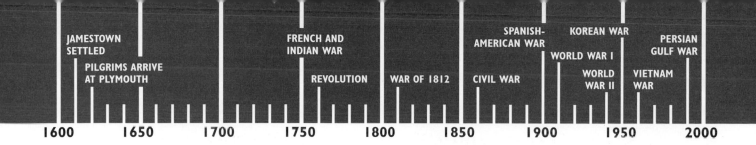

1600	1650	1700	1750	1800	1850	1900	1950	2000	

JAMESTOWN SETTLED

PILGRIMS ARRIVE AT PLYMOUTH

FRENCH AND INDIAN WAR

REVOLUTION

WAR OF 1812

CIVIL WAR

SPANISH-AMERICAN WAR

WORLD WAR I

KOREAN WAR

WORLD WAR II

VIETNAM WAR

PERSIAN GULF WAR

- Born about 1585, a member of the Pawtuxet tribe
- Arranged the first treaty between colonists and Native Americans
- Helped the Pilgrims survive
- Died in November 1622, in Cape Cod, Massachusetts

When the *Mayflower* dropped anchor off Plymouth in December 1620, the Pilgrims and others on board did not know how to survive in the harsh New England climate. Half of the 102 settlers died during that first winter.

In the spring, Squanto came to them. He spoke English and wanted to help. As an interpreter, he arranged a treaty of friendship between the Plymouth Colony and the Wampanoag tribe. Squanto showed the settlers how to fish. He brought them the seeds of foods that they had never seen before—corn, pumpkins, and squash—and showed them how to grow these crops.

With Squanto's help, the colony survived. In December 1621, the grateful Pilgrims held a great harvest festival: the first Thanksgiving.

The Pilgrims arrive at Plymouth in 1620.

The first Thanksgiving.

SQUANTO'S EXPERIENCE IN ENGLAND

In 1605, Squanto met English explorers and returned to England with them. It was from them that he learned to speak English. Squanto did not return to New England until 1614, when he helped Captain John Smith explore and map the coastline.

SOLD INTO SLAVERY

In 1615, Squanto and 30 other Indians were seized by a slave trader and sold in Spain as slaves. Squanto managed to escape and make his way to England. He arrived back in New England just in time to aid the Pilgrims. A year after the harvest festival, while helping the Pilgrims explore Cape Cod, he became ill and died.

UPDATE

The first nationwide celebration of Thanksgiving was proclaimed by President George Washington on November 26, 1789. Thanksgiving did not become a yearly national holiday until President Abraham Lincoln proclaimed it in 1863. And in 1941, Congress set the date as the fourth Thursday in November.

ANNE HUTCHINSON

CHAMPION OF RELIGIOUS FREEDOM

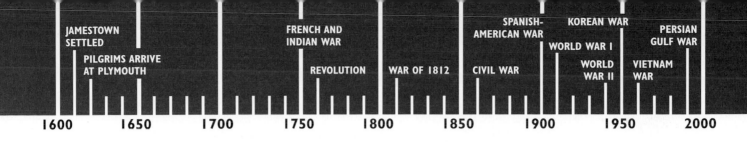

JAMESTOWN SETTLED				FRENCH AND INDIAN WAR				SPANISH-AMERICAN WAR	KOREAN WAR
	PILGRIMS ARRIVE AT PLYMOUTH							WORLD WAR I	PERSIAN GULF WAR
				REVOLUTION	WAR OF 1812	CIVIL WAR		WORLD WAR II	VIETNAM WAR

1600   1650   1700   1750   1800   1850   1900   1950   2000

- **Born in 1591, in Lincolnshire, England**
- **Banished from Massachusetts Bay Colony for her religious teachings**
- **Helped found the colony of Rhode Island**
- **Killed in an Indian raid in August 1643, in Long Island, New York**

Anne Hutchinson was one of the first Americans to stand up for the cause of religious freedom—the right to worship without government interference.

The murder of Anne Hutchinson.

Hutchinson and her husband, William, migrated to New England in 1634, four years after the founding of Massachusetts Bay Colony. She soon attracted a large following for her discussions of religion. Even ministers and government officials came to the meetings in her home.

But the colony was ruled by leaders of the Puritan Church who came to feel that Hutchinson's teachings were undermining their authority. She was put on trial in 1637 and banished from Massachusetts Bay Colony. With some of her followers, she fled to Rhode Island and started a new town on the island of Aquidneck.

HUTCHINSON'S COURAGE

After her trial, Anne Hutchinson was given the chance to recant—to say that her teachings were wrong. When she refused to do this, she was banned from the Puritan Church.

RHODE ISLAND

When Hutchinson and her followers arrived in Rhode Island, they were welcomed by Roger Williams. He had also been banished from Massachusetts Bay Colony for insisting on freedom of religion. Rhode Island quickly became a haven for settlers who had been punished for their religious beliefs. In 1644, England recognized the new colony and its charter, which granted religious freedom.

Roger Williams is accepted by the Narragansett of present-day Rhode Island.

WILLIAM PENN

FOUNDER OF PENNSYLVANIA AND DELAWARE

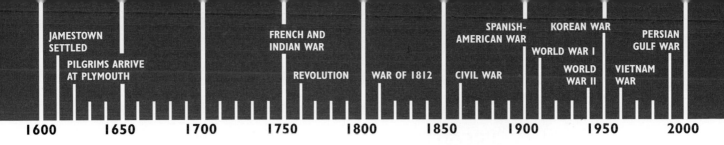

JAMESTOWN SETTLED		FRENCH AND INDIAN WAR			SPANISH-AMERICAN WAR	KOREAN WAR		PERSIAN GULF WAR

PILGRIMS ARRIVE AT PLYMOUTH · REVOLUTION · WAR OF 1812 · CIVIL WAR · WORLD WAR I · WORLD WAR II · VIETNAM WAR

1600   1650   1700   1750   1800   1850   1900   1950   2000

- Born on October 14, 1644, in London, England
- Imprisoned for his religious views
- Worked for peaceful relations with Native Americans
- Died on July 30, 1718, in Ruscombe, England

William Penn believed that all religions should be tolerated. He came to this belief the hard way. As a young man, he gave up a promising government career and joined the Religious Society of Friends, or Quakers. He was thrown into English prisons three times for preaching the unpopular Quaker beliefs.

Penn's life changed dramatically in 1681. King Charles II of England owed Penn's father a large sum of money. To repay the debt, Penn asked instead for land in the American colonies, to found a Quaker colony. The king granted a huge tract of land, naming it Pennsylvania, after William's father. Present-day Delaware was added a year later. Between 1682 and 1684, Penn established his colony, offering free land to settlers of every religion. He called it his Holy Experiment. This promise of religious tolerance made Pennsylvania one of the most successful colonies.

The king's deed to William Penn.

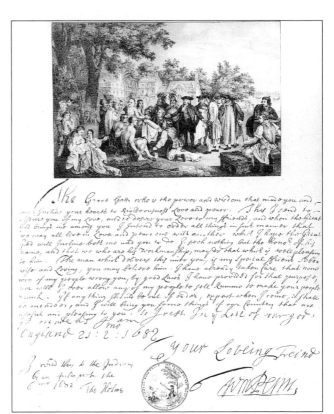

William Penn's handwritten treaty of friendship with the Indians.

PHILADELPHIA

When William Penn arrived in America, he established the city of Philadelphia, a name that means "brotherly love." He laid out the streets in a grid pattern, crossing at right angles. Many other major American cities later followed this plan.

QUAKERS AND NATIVE AMERICANS

Penn and his agents visited every Native-American tribe in Pennsylvania Colony and established treaties of friendship. The Quakers were pacifists—they did not believe in warfare or violence of any kind. Still, many of the settlers were so concerned about possible Indian attacks that they insisted on their right to use weapons to defend themselves.

15

DANIEL BOONE

FRONTIERSMAN AND EXPLORER

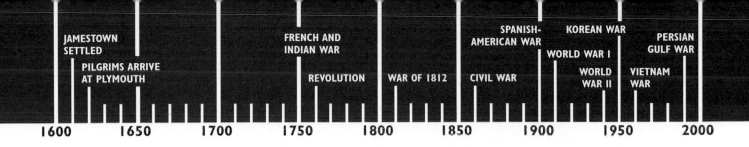

- **Born on November 2, 1734, near present-day Reading, Pennsylvania**
- **Explored the lands west of the Appalachian Mountains**
- **Opened the Wilderness Road through the Cumberland Gap into Kentucky**
- **Died on September 26, 1820, in St. Charles County, Missouri**

Of all America's frontier heroes, Daniel Boone is the most famous. He helped lead settlement westward beyond the Appalachian Mountains. And his feats of courage became legendary.

As a boy, Boone loved to hunt and to wander the wilderness. He became a skilled woodsman and a crack shot. He was thrilled when his family moved to the frontier of North Carolina in 1750. Daniel Boone never went to school, although he did learn to read and write.

Boone worked as a blacksmith and a wagon driver, or teamster. In 1755, during the French and Indian War, he was a horse-team driver for a British and colonial force that was sent to drive the French from the Pennsylvania frontier. The French and their Native-American allies ambushed the force, killing some and capturing many, including a young colonel named George Washington. Boone, however, managed to escape.

After the war, Boone began to explore the wilderness beyond the Appalachian Mountains. With a handful of hunters, he spent two years in what is now Kentucky. When he returned to North Carolina, in 1771, he brought back stories of the beautiful country beyond the mountains, a land with rich soil for farming and great herds of deer and bison.

After U.S. independence, he served for a time in the government of Virginia and later was a sheriff and a surveyor. In 1799, he moved his family again, this time west of the Mississippi into Missouri. He remained here until his death at the age of 86.

THE LONG HUNTERS

Daniel Boone was the most famous of a courageous band of men known as the Long Hunters. The name came from their being away from home for such long periods. While they were away, their wives and children tended the family farms. Boone's wife, Rebecca, was nearly as good a shot as he was.

SAVING BOONESBOROUGH

In 1778, Boone was captured by the Shawnees, who adopted him into their tribe. When he heard that the Shawnees planned to attack the fort of Boonesborough, he managed to escape in time to warn the settlers. About 400 Shawnees surrounded the fort, but Boone and some 50 men and boys held them at bay. The Shawnees finally gave up and left Boonesborough in peace.

JEMIMA'S ESCAPE

In 1776, Boone's 14-year-old daughter, Jemima, and two of her friends were kidnapped by Native-American warriors. The frightened girls managed to mark the trail by tearing off bits of cloth from their dresses. Boone followed the scraps for three days and rescued the girls unharmed.

UPDATE

Daniel Boone was the model for the hero in James Fennimore Cooper's (1789-1850) *Leatherstocking Tales* about the American frontier. The most popular of the novels were *The Pathfinder*, *The Last of the Mohicans*, and *The Deerslayer*. Movies have been based on all of these books.

The American Revolution

By the end of the French and Indian War, in 1763, the Thirteen Colonies were prosperous and growing rapidly. But the war had been costly to Great Britain. The king and parliament decided that the colonies should help to pay these costs. They tried a series of new taxes and began to govern the colonies more closely.

The colonists were angered. They felt that the taxes were unfair, because the colonies had not voted for them—they had been given no representatives in Parliament. They also disliked the stricter control over their affairs. Between 1763 and 1773, the colonies and Britain grew further apart. The colonists formed patriotic groups—the Sons of Liberty and Daughters of Liberty—to demand their rights. When some of these Patriots dumped British tea into Boston Harbor, in protest against a new tax on tea, the British clamped down even harder. In 1775, the first fighting of the Revolution began at Lexington and Concord in Massachusetts. The Declaration of Independence was signed in 1776.

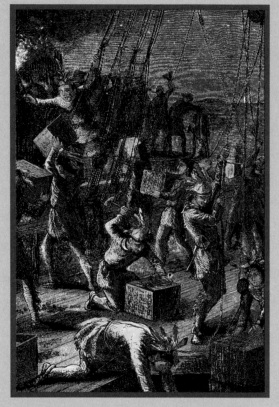

Patriots destroy tea in the Boston Harbor.

Great Britain was the world's mightiest nation, with a powerful army and a navy that ruled the seas. How could the Americans hope to win? One problem for King George III was that many of his subjects did not want to fight against people they considered to be fellow citizens. To beef up his army, the king had to hire 30,000 German soldiers, the Hessians. But the Americans, fighting for their homes and their liberty, were able to overcome the odds against them. And even though African Americans were not accepted as free citizens, more than 7,000 fought in the Continental Army and Navy.

The War for Independence—the American Revolution—dragged on for eight years (1775-1783). Time after time, the leadership of General George Washington saved the young country from defeat. The Americans won independence in 1783. Six years later, the Constitution was written, establishing the form of government that the United States has today.

Many men and women were heroes during the Revolution. You will meet a few of them on the pages that follow.

C H R O N O L O G Y

1756 The French and Indian War begins

1763 The French and Indian War ends

1770 The Boston Massacre takes place

1773 Patriots dump tea into Boston Harbor

1775 Paul Revere alerts the Minutemen that British soldiers are coming to Lexington

1775 Fighting between the British and the colonists begins at Lexington and Concord

1775 Patrick Henry addresses the Virginia Convention

1775 The American Revolution begins

1776 The Declaration of Independence is signed

1778 Molly Pitcher fights at the Battle of Monmouth

1779 John Paul Jones fights the British from his ship *Bonhomme Richard*

1780 Francis Marion forms Marion's Brigade

1781 The American Revolution ends with Cornwallis's surrender at Yorktown

1787 The Constitution is written

1788 Patrick Henry opposes adoption of the Constitution

1789 The Constitution is adopted and George Washington becomes the nation's first president

PAUL REVERE

PATRIOT AND CRAFTSMAN

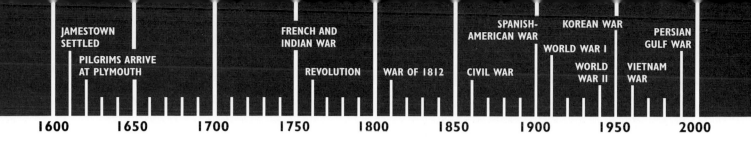

				SPANISH-	KOREAN WAR	
JAMESTOWN SETTLED		FRENCH AND INDIAN WAR		AMERICAN WAR		PERSIAN GULF WAR
PILGRIMS ARRIVE AT PLYMOUTH		REVOLUTION	WAR OF 1812	CIVIL WAR	WORLD WAR I	WORLD WAR II	VIETNAM WAR

1600   1650   1700   1750   1800   1850   1900   1950   2000

- **Born on January 1, 1735, in Boston, Massachusetts**
- **One of the leaders of the Boston Tea Party**
- **Warned Patriots of the British advance to Lexington**
- **Died on May 10, 1818, in Boston**

Late on the night of April 18, 1775, Paul Revere stood by his horse, staring across the river at Boston, which was controlled by the British. When he saw a lantern flash in the bell tower of Old North Church, he set off on the most famous ride in American history. With another Patriot, Billy Dawes, Revere rode through the countryside, pounding on farmhouse doors and shouting his warning that a British regiment was heading toward Lexington and Concord. The British had planned a surprise, to seize the patriots' weapons and capture two of their leaders: Samuel Adams and John Hancock. Alerted by Revere, the patriot militia—the "Minutemen"—were ready. The battles that followed at Lexington and Concord marked the start of the American Revolution

Paul Revere's "midnight ride" helped to make him one of the most famous heroes of America's War for Independence. But his fame was built on more than that heroic ride.

When he was 19 years old, his father died, and Paul Revere took over the family's silversmith business. He soon became known for his fine work in silver, pewter, and gold. As the Thirteen Colonies drifted into conflict with British colonial rule, Revere became one of the early leaders of the Sons of Liberty. In 1773, he was one of the Patriots who led the Boston Tea Party. Dressed as Native Americans, they boarded British ships in Boston Harbor and dumped the casks of tea overboard to protest the tax on tea. Revere also served as an express rider for the Patriots, carrying news and messages to other colonies.

After independence was won, Revere returned to his silversmith business. He also opened a large foundry for manufacturing gunpowder, cannons, and copper church bells. In addition, he was a pioneer in using copper sheeting to protect the bottoms of ships. One of the first ships on which he used this method was the U.S.S. *Constitution*.

Paul Revere's midnight ride.

PAUL REVERE, DENTIST

There were no dentists in eighteenth century America. When a toothache became bad enough, the sufferer simply had the tooth pulled out, usually by a barber. Many people in Boston turned to Paul Revere to fashion a set of false teeth.

PATRIOT INFORMATION

Revere used his skill as an engraver to help the Patriot cause. When British soldiers shot and killed five colonists in 1770, Revere made an engraving of what became known as the "Boston Massacre." The engraving was reproduced throughout the colonies and helped to unite Americans against British rule. He also engraved the first American money.

21

PATRICK HENRY

PATRIOT LEADER AND ORATOR

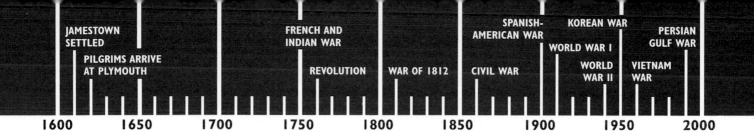

JAMESTOWN SETTLED

PILGRIMS ARRIVE AT PLYMOUTH

FRENCH AND INDIAN WAR

REVOLUTION

WAR OF 1812

CIVIL WAR

SPANISH-AMERICAN WAR

KOREAN WAR

WORLD WAR I

WORLD WAR II

VIETNAM WAR

PERSIAN GULF WAR

1600   1650   1700   1750   1800   1850   1900   1950   2000

- **Born on May 29, 1736, in Hanover County, Virginia**
- **One of the first leaders of the Patriot cause**
- **Delegate to the Continental Congress**
- **Five-term governor of Virginia**
- **Died on June 6, 1799, in Charlotte County, Virginia**

Patrick Henry was known as a firebrand—a man who could stir others to action by his powerful speeches. His eloquence as an orator helped convince the colonists to declare their independence from Great Britain.

In the spring of 1775, the American colonists were not sure what action to take against British rule. Many felt that taking up arms against Great Britain would be treason. In the most famous speech of the Revolution, Henry urged the Virginia Convention to take the bold action of declaring independence and then fighting to achieve it. "Is life so dear, or peace so sweet, as to be purchased at the price of chains and slavery?" he demanded. "Forbid it, Almighty God! I know not what course others may take, but, as for me, give me liberty or give me death!"

Henry's stirring speech was soon printed and distributed everywhere. It helped create the mood that led to the Declaration of Independence a year later.

As an independent state, Virginia elected Patrick Henry as its first governor. He served a total of five terms at different times.

Patrick Henry addresses the Continental Congress.

EARLY STRUGGLES

Success did not come easily to Patrick Henry. As a young man, he failed as a farmer and then as a store owner. He finally taught himself law and began a brilliant career, in which he won most of his more than 1,000 cases.

PATRICK HENRY AND THE CONSTITUTION

In 1788, Henry opposed the adoption of the Constitution, because he feared that a strong central government would limit individual rights. After it was approved, he urged the adoption of the first ten amendments—the Bill of Rights—to protect those rights.

LATER YEARS

In his later years, poor health forced Henry to retire from public service. He turned down many important posts, including U.S. secretary of state and chief justice of the Supreme Court. He finally agreed to run for the Senate. Henry won the election, but died before taking office.

MOLLY PITCHER

HERO OF THE BATTLE OF MONMOUTH

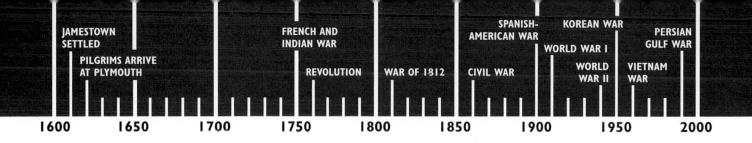

						SPANISH-AMERICAN WAR	KOREAN WAR	
JAMESTOWN SETTLED			FRENCH AND INDIAN WAR				WORLD WAR I	PERSIAN GULF WAR
	PILGRIMS ARRIVE AT PLYMOUTH			REVOLUTION	WAR OF 1812	CIVIL WAR	WORLD WAR II	VIETNAM WAR

1600   1650   1700   1750   1800   1850   1900   1950   2000

- **Born on October 13, 1754, in Trenton, New Jersey**
- **Earned her nickname on the battlefield**
- **Awarded a pension for her bravery**
- **Died on January 22, 1832, in Carlisle, Pennsylvania**

June 28, 1778, was a hot, muggy day in New Jersey. In the steamy dawn, General George Washington's Continental Army took up positions at the village of Monmouth Courthouse to face the British redcoats. One of the heroes in the day-long battle that followed was a young woman who is known as Molly Pitcher.

Her real name was Mary Ludwig Hays. She worked as a servant in Carlisle, Pennsylvania. When

General George Washington.

her husband, John Hays, joined the 7th Pennsylvania Regiment, Mary went along with him, as many soldiers' wives did. The women cooked, washed, searched for food, and tended the sick and wounded.

Through the blistering heat one afternoon, the cannons kept up a steady bombardment. To help the exhausted gunners and the wounded, Mary began carrying pitchers of water to the front lines. This is when grateful soldiers gave her the nickname.

According to legend, Molly Pitcher's husband collapsed from the heat, and she took over his post—as artillery man—loading the cannon until the battle was over. The Patriots won a close victory at Monmouth that day, and they also gained a new hero.

A HEROINE'S REWARD

Many people doubted that Molly Pitcher had actually fought in the battle at Monmouth. But in 1822, Pennsylvania awarded her a pension of $40 a year for her heroism. One of the soldiers who wrote on her behalf told of seeing her loading the cannon. At one point, he recalled, with her feet spread wide apart to reach a cartridge, a cannon ball "shot from the enemy passed directly between her legs without doing any other damage than carrying away all the lower part of her petticoat."

25

FRANCIS MARION

REVOLUTIONARY WAR OFFICER

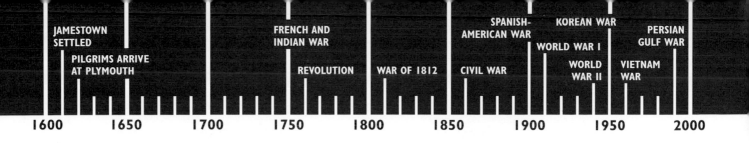

JAMESTOWN SETTLED		FRENCH AND INDIAN WAR			SPANISH-AMERICAN WAR	KOREAN WAR	PERSIAN GULF WAR
PILGRIMS ARRIVE AT PLYMOUTH					WORLD WAR I		
		REVOLUTION	WAR OF 1812	CIVIL WAR		WORLD WAR II	VIETNAM WAR

1600   1650   1700   1750   1800   1850   1900   1950   2000

- **Born about 1732 in Berkeley County, South Carolina**
- **Developed hit-and-run battle tactics**
- **Known as the "Swamp Fox"**
- **Died on February 27, 1795, in Berkeley County**

Francis Marion and his troops surprise a British wagon train.

In 1780, the war was going badly for the Patriots, especially in the South. When the British captured Charleston, South Carolina, Colonel Francis Marion was one of the few Continental officers who escaped. Marion knew something had to be done. He gathered about 200 of the best men he could find and formed Marion's Brigade.

The colonel counted on speed and daring to fight the larger British forces. He moved his band

Francis Marion.

through South Carolina's thick woods and swamps. From there, they would launch a surprise attack on the redcoats, then disappear back into the swamps. For nearly two years, Marion and a few other leaders kept the Continental hopes alive in the South. Marion was promoted to brigadier general and received the thanks of Congress. By late 1781, larger Continental forces had arrived. Marion's Brigade helped win the final battles of the war. Marion later served in his state's senate and then became commander of a fort in Charleston Harbor.

PRAISE FROM THE ENEMY

The most feared British officer in the South was Colonel Banastre Tarleton. Tarleton was determined to capture Marion. But every time the British seemed to have Marion cornered, he would slip away into the murky swamps. "As for the damned old fox," Tarleton exclaimed, "the devil himself could not catch him." From then on, Marion was known as the Swamp Fox.

IMPROVISING

In one battle, Marion's Brigade surrounded a British force, but the British were protected by a high log stockade. Marion's men, being handy with axes, built a wooden tower. From the tower, the sharpshooters had clear aim at the stockade. The British were forced to surrender.

JOHN PAUL JONES

NAVAL COMMANDER IN THE REVOLUTIONARY WAR

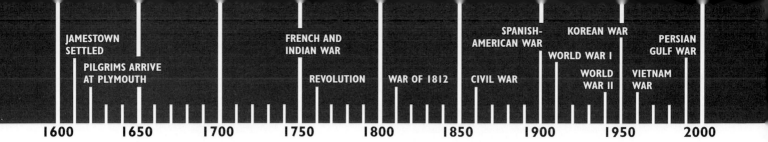

| JAMESTOWN SETTLED | | FRENCH AND INDIAN WAR | | | | SPANISH-AMERICAN WAR | KOREAN WAR | PERSIAN GULF WAR |
| PILGRIMS ARRIVE AT PLYMOUTH | | | REVOLUTION | WAR OF 1812 | CIVIL WAR | WORLD WAR I | WORLD WAR II | VIETNAM WAR |

| 1600 | 1650 | 1700 | 1750 | 1800 | 1850 | 1900 | 1950 | 2000 |

- Born on July 6, 1747, in Scotland
- Carried the war to the shores of Great Britain
- Won the most famous sea battle of the war
- Died on July 18, 1792, in Paris, France

One of the greatest sea battles in American history took place on September 23, 1779, off the coast of England. The American ship *Bonhomme Richard* was outmanned and outgunned by the British warship *Serapis*. But the *Bonhomme Richard* was commanded by John Paul Jones, and Jones had no intention of losing.

John Paul Jones makes his stand on the *Bonhomme Richard*.

Jones had already proved his brilliance as a naval commander, capturing more than a dozen British merchant ships. But as night fell on September 23, the *Bonhomme Richard* was taking a tremendous beating from the heavy cannon of the *Serapis*. Jones managed to move his ship close to the *Serapis*, and then lashed them together. When the British commander asked Jones if he was ready to surrender, he gave the famous reply, "I have not yet begun to fight!" The battle continued hand-to-hand into the night, until the British were finally forced to surrender. Jones transferred his men to the captured ship and allowed the badly damaged *Bonhomme Richard* to sink. The victory gave a great boost to the American people and their young Continental Navy.

The *Serapis* and *Bonhomme Richard* at war.

A NEW NAME

This naval commander's name was really John Paul. He went to sea at age 12. At 22, he became captain of a British merchant ship. In 1773, he put down a mutiny by running his sword through the ringleader. To avoid a trial, he fled to America, where he added Jones to his name. In 1779, he named his ship *Bonhomme Richard* in honor of Benjamin Franklin, creator of *Poor Richard's Almanac*.

THE FIRST NAVY FLAG

Jones sailed the first Continental Navy ship to fly the Grand Union flag.

UPDATE

After the Revolutionary War, the Continental Navy was dissolved. John Paul Jones became an admiral in the Russian Navy and then retired to France, where he died. His unmarked grave was rediscovered in 1905. His remains were returned to America by an honor fleet and placed in a crypt in the chapel of the U.S. Naval Academy, in Annapolis, Maryland.

29

The Early United States

Even before the United States had won independence from Great Britain, settlers began pouring into the country's frontier regions. Within 20 years, 4 new states—Vermont, Ohio, Kentucky, and Tennessee—had been added to the original 13. But as pioneers pushed westward, they ran into opposition from two sources: The Native American tribes, and the British in control of Canada.

The determined Americans were not about to give in. They pushed the Native Americans farther and farther west. Many of the tribes fought back, and there were years of frontier raids, ambushes, and pitched battles.

During the same years, relations between the young United States and Great Britain grew worse. Many Americans came to believe that another war was needed to settle things with the British, end their help to the Indians, and maybe gain control of Canada. In June 1812, Congress declared war against Great Britain,

British ships blockade the Chesapeake Bay during the War of 1812.

and the War of 1812 began. Many of the Native-American tribes fought on the British side. The war lasted until 1815. Even though the United States gained nothing from it, the heroes who emerged gave Americans a new sense of national pride and unity.

After the War of 1812, American settlers continued to push westward. By 1850, the nation had grown to 31 states, 8 of them west of the Mississippi River. The territory of the United States now extended from the Atlantic Ocean to the Pacific.

The United States was changing in many other ways, too. New factories began to produce goods on a large scale. Steamboats piled the waterways, and railroads speeded the movement of goods and people. Some Americans wanted to make the United States a better nation. They began movements to esablish schools, to grant women the right to vote, and to end slavery.

C H R O N O L O G Y

1794 Dolley Payne Todd marries James Madison

1804 Stephen Decatur leads a raid into Tripoli harbor

1806–1807 Oliver Hazard Perry fights against the Barbary pirates

1811 Native Americans are defeated at the Battle of Tippecanoe

1812 U.S. Congress declares war against Great Britain. The War of 1812 lasts for three years

October—Stephen Decatur wins the first naval victory of the War of 1812

1813 Oliver Hazard Perry leads American ships to victory at the Battle of Lake Erie

1815 Stephen Decatur's ship is captured by the British

1815 Andrew Jackson leads troops during the Battle of New Orleans

1815 Dolley Madison saves important documents from the White House before it is set on fire by the British

TECUMSEH

SHAWNEE LEADER, WAR CHIEF, AND ORATOR

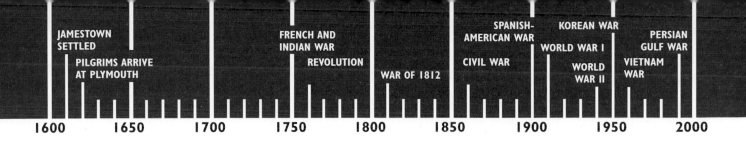

JAMESTOWN SETTLED

PILGRIMS ARRIVE AT PLYMOUTH

FRENCH AND INDIAN WAR

REVOLUTION

WAR OF 1812

SPANISH-AMERICAN WAR

CIVIL WAR

KOREAN WAR

WORLD WAR I

WORLD WAR II

PERSIAN GULF WAR

VIETNAM WAR

1600   1650   1700   1750   1800   1850   1900   1950   2000

- **Born in March 1768, near present-day Dayton, Ohio**
- **Respected for his kindness, intelligence, courage, and speaking skill**
- **Organized a union of tribes**
- **Killed on October 5, 1813, at the Battle of the Thames, in Ontario, Canada**

After the Revolutionary War, American settlers began pouring into the western territories of Ohio and Indiana. The Shawnee chief Tecumseh saw that this westward movement would mean the end of the Native-American way of life. In the early 1800s, he began organizing a large union of tribes to stop the settlers' advance.

Tecumseh was aided by his brother, Tenskwatawa, a religious mystic called the Prophet. They founded a settlement in Indiana Territory called Prophetstown, and Tecumseh used his great skill as a speaker to persuade thousands of Indians from the east to join them. But in November 1811, while Tecumseh was traveling in the South, an American force marched on Prophetstown. In the battle that followed, known as the Battle of Tippecanoe, the

Tecumseh confronts General William Henry Harrison.

Native Americans were forced to flee, and their settlement was destroyed.

Outraged by the attack, Tecumseh sided with the British when the War of 1812 began. Leading as many as 15,000 warriors, he won several battles but was killed during the Battle of the Thames, in Ontario, Canada. Tecumseh's death ended one of the most ambitious attempts in history to unite all the tribes.

Tecumseh dies during the Battle of the Thames.

TECUMSEH'S EDUCATION

Tecumseh learned to read and write, and he studied history, with the help of a white woman, Rebecca Galloway. They fell in love and she agreed to marry him if he would give up his Indian ways. Tecumseh decided he could not do that.

TECUMSEH AND HARRISON

Tecumseh's chief opponent was General William Henry Harrison, the governor of Indiana Territory. It was Harrison who planned and led the Battle of Tippecanoe. And it was Harrison who led the American force in the Battle of the Thames, which cost Tecumseh his life.

STEPHEN DECATUR

NAVAL OFFICER AND HERO OF TWO WARS

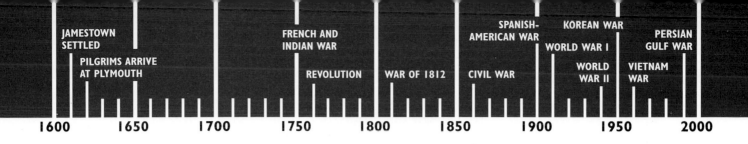

JAMESTOWN SETTLED

PILGRIMS ARRIVE AT PLYMOUTH

FRENCH AND INDIAN WAR

REVOLUTION

WAR OF 1812

SPANISH-AMERICAN WAR

CIVIL WAR

KOREAN WAR

WORLD WAR I

WORLD WAR II

VIETNAM WAR

PERSIAN GULF WAR

1600   1650   1700   1750   1800   1850   1900   1950   2000

- **Born January 5, 1779, in Sinepuxent, Maryland**
- **Led a daring raid against the Barbary pirates**
- **Won a dramatic naval victory in the War of 1812**
- **Killed in a duel on March 22, 1820, in Maryland**

For many years, the kingdoms on the Barbary Coast of North Africa, on the Mediterranean Sea, had made a living by piracy. They captured American and European ships, then held the crews for ransom. President Thomas Jefferson sent a fleet of warships to try to put the Barbary pirates out of business. In February 1804, Lieutenant Stephen Decatur led a bold night raid into the pirate harbor of Tripoli, Libya. With just a handful of men, he set fire to a captured American ship and returned safely to his own ship. The raid was called "the most bold and daring naval act of the age."

Decatur displayed his heroism again in the War of 1812. In command of the warship *United States*, he won America's first naval victory of the war, in October 1812. He also captured a British warship and brought it intact into a Connecticut harbor. The episode showed that the American Navy could hold its own against the much larger British fleet.

THE WAR'S LAST PRISONER

Stephen Decatur suffered only one naval defeat. In January 1815, his ship, the *President*, was captured by the British, and he was taken prisoner. The war had actually ended two weeks earlier, when a peace treaty was signed, but people on the ships at sea had not yet received the news.

THE END OF THE BARBARY PIRATES

In 1815, Decatur returned to the Mediterranean to put an end to the Barbary pirates. After sinking two pirate ships and killing their most powerful leader, Decatur accepted the pirates' surrender.

DEATH IN A DUEL

In 1820 Decatur was challenged to a duel by a former navy commander, James Barron. Decatur had presided over Barron's court martial, and Barron charged that the outcome was unfair. Barron shot Decatur to death in the duel.

Stephen Decatur set fire to the *Philadelphia* in Tripoli harbor.

OLIVER HAZARD PERRY

NAVAL OFFICER AND HERO OF THE BATTLE OF LAKE ERIE

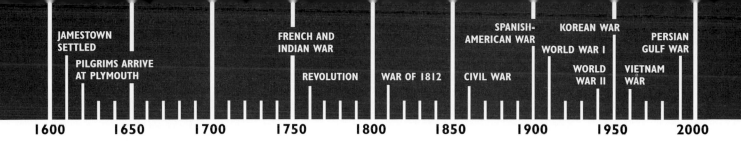

JAMESTOWN SETTLED

PILGRIMS ARRIVE AT PLYMOUTH

FRENCH AND INDIAN WAR

REVOLUTION

WAR OF 1812

CIVIL WAR

SPANISH-AMERICAN WAR

WORLD WAR I

KOREAN WAR

WORLD WAR II

VIETNAM WAR

PERSIAN GULF WAR

1600   1650   1700   1750   1800   1850   1900   1950   2000

- Born on August 23, 1785, in South Kingstown, Rhode Island
- Fought against the Barbary pirates, 1806-1807
- Defeated a British fleet in the Battle of Lake Erie
- Died of yellow fever on August 23, 1819, in Venezuela

Early in the War of 1812, Navy Commander Oliver Hazard Perry was ordered to take control of Lake Erie from the British. Eager for action, Perry rushed to his post, only to discover that there were no ships to command.

For more than six months, Perry and his men worked furiously to assemble a fleet of nine small ships. Then they took up position at Put-in-Bay and waited for the British. The Battle of Lake Erie raged through the day of September 10, 1813. Perry's flagship, the *Lawrence*, was blown apart, but he

The Battle of Lake Erie.

made his way to the *Niagara* and continued to lead the fight, forcing his way through the line of British ships. The British were forced to surrender by nightfall, giving the United States control of the lake. In a famous message, Perry wrote to the army commander on shore: "We have met the enemy and they are ours." The victory was one of the war's bright spots for Americans and added to the nation's proud naval tradition.

CREATING A FLEET

To create his fleet, Perry and his men built five ships, using every piece of material they could find, including barn doors and hinges. The other ships were brought from Lake Ontario; they were moved overland to get past Niagara Falls.

HONORING A FRIEND

Perry named his flagship the *Lawrence* in honor of his friend James Lawrence, who had been killed in a naval battle a few months earlier. For his battle-flag motto, Perry chose Lawrence's dying words, "Don't give up the ship!" The motto soon became standard in the U.S. Navy.

AFRICAN AMERICANS ON LAKE ERIE

About a fourth of the men who served under Perry were African Americans. Their courage at the Battle of Lake Erie led Perry to remark, "The color of a man's skin is no more an indication of his worth than the cut and trimmings of his coat."

DOLLEY MADISON

FIRST LADY AND HEROINE OF THE WAR OF 1812

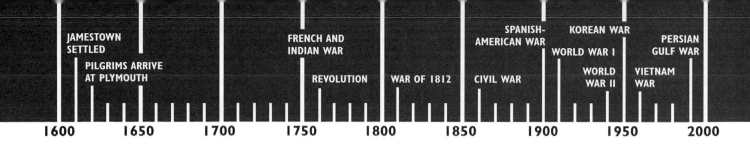

JAMESTOWN SETTLED

PILGRIMS ARRIVE AT PLYMOUTH

FRENCH AND INDIAN WAR

REVOLUTION

WAR OF 1812

CIVIL WAR

SPANISH-AMERICAN WAR

KOREAN WAR

WORLD WAR I

WORLD WAR II

VIETNAM WAR

PERSIAN GULF WAR

1600   1650   1700   1750   1800   1850   1900   1950   2000

- **Born May 10, 1768, in Guilford County, North Carolina**
- **Directed White House social functions for 16 years**
- **Saved valuable items when the White House was burned**
- **Died July 12, 1849, in Washington, D.C.**

In the last months of the War of 1812, the American cause was going badly. A British force had raided many important coastal towns and then marched on Washington, D.C. President James Madison left to be with whatever defending army was available to try to stop the British. That meant First Lady Dolley Payne Todd Madison was alone in the White House with a few servants.

Through a telescope, Dolley Madison watched the enemy advance. Realizing that the British would not be stopped, she quickly gathered the most important of her husband's papers. Then, remembering a promise she had made to George Washington's grandson, she had a famous portrait of Washington removed from its frame and carried it with her as she fled.

The British troops stormed into the city and set fire to both the Capitol and the White House. A fierce storm saved the buildings from complete destruction, and the Madisons escaped. In one of the nation's darkest hours, Dolley Madison had provided a courageous spark of hope.

WHITE HOUSE HOSTESS

Dolley Madison served as hostess of White House functions longer than any other woman—a total of 16 years. Before James Madison was elected president in 1808, he had served as President Thomas Jefferson's secretary of state. Since Jefferson was a widower, he persuaded Dolley Madison to take charge of all White House social functions. As White House hostess, she was noted for her graciousness.

AN EARLIER TRAGEDY

In 1790, when she was 22, Dolley Payne married John Todd, Jr. Tragedy struck the family in 1793 when Todd and one of their two infant children died of yellow fever. Dolley slowly recovered from the loss and married James Madison in 1794.

British troops burn and capture Washington, D.C.

The Civil War Era

One of the inventions that changed the nation in the early 1800s was Eli Whitney's cotton gin. With this device, cotton could be cleaned of its seeds 50 times faster than by hand. Many of the larger plantations in the South turned to cotton growing, and the region soon became the world's largest supplier of cotton. The boom in cotton, however, increased plantation owners' demand for slaves to work the fields.

The Battle of Corinth.

At the time the U.S. Constitution was written, many of the Founders of the nation believed that slavery would slowly die out. Instead, while slavery was ended in the North, it became more deeply entrenched in the South.

North and South gradually divided over the slavery issue. In the 1830s, some people in the North began forming abolitionist, or anti-slavery, societies. They were soon joined by free African Americans. Most northerners said that slavery in the South was not their concern. But the abolitionists continued to speak out, even when they were attacked by angry mobs.

In 1860-1861, 11 southern states seceded from, or left, the Union of States to form the Confederate States of America. The Civil War between the Union (North) and the Confederacy (South) lasted from April 1861 to April 1865. No war, before or since, has claimed so many American lives.

There was great heroism on both sides in this struggle. Most southerners did not own slaves, but they felt that they were fighting for their homes and their way of life. Northerners were fighting at first to preserve the Union and the Constitution. Then, after President Abraham Lincoln issued the Emancipation Proclamation, which freed the slaves, northerners felt they had another great cause: ending slavery in America.

C H R O N O L O G Y

1838 Frederick Douglass escapes slavery and becomes free

1845 Douglass's autobiography, *Narrative of the Life of Frederick Douglass* is published

1849 Harriet Tubman escapes slavery and becomes free

1859 John Brown leads a raid on Harpers Ferry, Virginia

1861 The Civil War begins

1862 Robert E. Lee is given command of the Army of Northern Virginia

1863 Harriet Tubman leads a Union force into Confederate territory

1863 General Lee and the South are defeated at the Battle of Gettysburg

1865 The Civil War ends after General Lee surrenders to General Ulysses S. Grant at Appomattox Court House, Virginia

1866 Grant is made a general of the U. S. Army

1868–1876 Grant serves as U. S. president

1881 Clara Barton becomes president of the new American National Red Cross

HARRIET TUBMAN

ABOLITIONIST

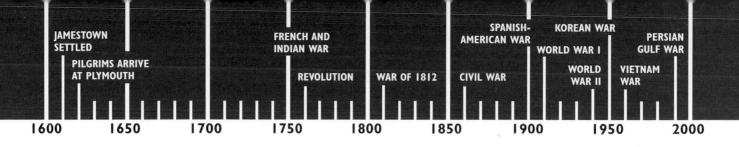

JAMESTOWN
SETTLED

PILGRIMS ARRIVE
AT PLYMOUTH

FRENCH AND
INDIAN WAR

REVOLUTION

WAR OF 1812

CIVIL WAR

SPANISH-
AMERICAN WAR

WORLD WAR I

WORLD
WAR II

KOREAN WAR

VIETNAM
WAR

PERSIAN
GULF WAR

1600   1650   1700   1750   1800   1850   1900   1950   2000

- Born a slave about 1820, in Dorchester County, Maryland
- Became a conductor on the Underground Railroad and led more than 300 slaves to freedom
- Served as a scout, spy, and nurse in the Civil War
- Died on March 10, 1913, in Auburn, New York

During the 1840s and 1850s, many slaves in the South found a new source of hope. It was called the Underground Railroad. It was not a real railroad but, rather, an informal network of people who hid escaped slaves and helped them on their dangerous journey to freedom in the North or in Canada. Both whites and African Americans helped on the Underground Railroad. Some served as "conductors," traveling to the South to help slaves escape.

Slaves are freed by Union Army soldiers.

Harriet Tubman was the most famous conductor on the Underground Railroad. She escaped slavery in 1849, but was forced to leave behind her husband, John Tubman, her parents, and the rest of her family. Freedom for herself was not enough for Harriet Tubman; she was determined that "my people must go free."

A strong woman with an iron will, she made 19 trips into the South, risking her life to help others find freedom in the North or in Canada. Bounty hunters were constantly after her, hoping for the reward—up to $40,000—for her capture. But Tubman always

avoided capture and led a total of more than 300 slaves to freedom, including her elderly parents.

During the Civil War, the government encouraged her to continue her work as the "Moses of her people." For more than three years, she served with Union forces in Florida and the Carolinas. She worked as a nurse, a cook, and a laundress. Tubman proved even more valuable as a scout and a spy. Accompanied by other African Americans, she made several trips behind Confederate lines, returning with vital information about the location of troops, ammunition depots, and slaves waiting to be liberated. In June 1863, she led a Union force on a daring raid deep into Confederate territory.

After the war, Tubman helped to establish schools in North Carolina for freed slaves. Later, she moved to Auburn, New York, where she set up a home for the elderly. After her death in 1913, the town continued to operate the home.

HARRIET TUBMAN AND JOHN BROWN

When Tubman was in Canada in 1858, she met John Brown, the fiery abolitionist who planned to begin a great slave revolt by raiding the federal arsenal at Harpers Ferry, Virginia. Because of her deep hatred of slavery, she helped him plan the ill-fated raid. In 1859, federal troops easily crushed Brown's small band. No slave revolt resulted, but the event did move the nation closer to war.

John Brown opposed slavery and fought for slaves' freedom.

FREDERICK DOUGLASS

ABOLITIONIST, JOURNALIST, AND GOVERNMENT OFFICIAL

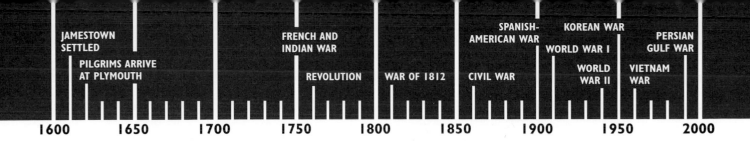

| | JAMESTOWN SETTLED | | | | FRENCH AND INDIAN WAR | | | | SPANISH-AMERICAN WAR | KOREAN WAR | | PERSIAN GULF WAR |
| | PILGRIMS ARRIVE AT PLYMOUTH | | | | REVOLUTION | WAR OF 1812 | CIVIL WAR | | WORLD WAR I | WORLD WAR II | VIETNAM WAR |

| 1600 | 1650 | 1700 | 1750 | 1800 | 1850 | 1900 | 1950 | 2000 |

- **Born in February 1817, in Tuckahoe, Maryland**
- **Escaped from slavery and became a leading abolitionist**
- **Recruited African-American troops during the Civil War**
- **Died on February 20, 1895, in Washington, D.C.**

Frederick Augustus Washington Baily learned to read and write while he was a household slave. After being sent to work as a plantation field hand, he escaped in 1838 and changed his name to Frederick Douglass.

In the early 1840s, Douglass discovered that he could move people with the power of his speeches. He joined the Massachusetts Anti-Slavery Society and became one of the most famous abolitionist speakers. His autobiography, *Narrative of the Life of Frederick Douglass*, was published in 1845. The book helped to strengthen anti-slavery feelings in the North and in Great Britain. He also founded and edited an anti-slavery newspaper, *The North Star*.

During the Civil War, Douglass pressured President Abraham Lincoln to abolish slavery. When the president issued the Emancipation Proclamation, Douglass began recruiting African Americans to serve in the Union Army.

A slave auction.

WHY HE WROTE

When Frederick Douglass began speaking for anti-slavery organizations, some people said that he was too well educated to have been a slave. To set the record straight, Douglass wrote his *Narrative*. No one ever doubted his bitter slave experience after that.

MINISTER TO HAITI

After the Civil War, Douglass was appointed to several government positions. From 1889 to 1891, he was the U.S. minister to Haiti—the first time an African American had been the country's representative to another nation.

Many African Americans were soldiers during the Civil War.

47

ROBERT E. LEE

SOLDIER AND THE LEADING CONFEDERATE GENERAL

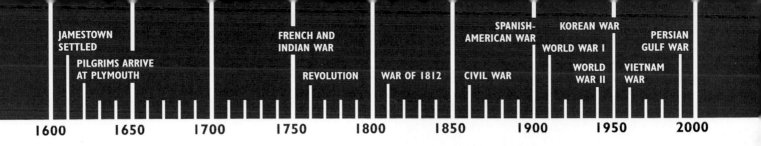

JAMESTOWN SETTLED		FRENCH AND INDIAN WAR			SPANISH-AMERICAN WAR	KOREAN WAR	PERSIAN GULF WAR
PILGRIMS ARRIVE AT PLYMOUTH		REVOLUTION	WAR OF 1812	CIVIL WAR	WORLD WAR I	WORLD WAR II	VIETNAM WAR

1600 1650 1700 1750 1800 1850 1900 1950 2000

- Born January 19, 1807, in Westmoreland County, Virginia
- Led Confederate forces in a series of spectacular battles
- Respected even by his enemies for his gallantry and skill
- Died October 12, 1870, in Lexington, Virginia

Robert E. Lee loved his country. He also hated slavery. But his strongest loyalty went to his native Virginia. So when Virginia joined the Confederacy, he too sided with the South. In 1862, he was placed in command of the Army of Northern Virginia. Over the next three years, General Lee proved himself to be the greatest strategist of the war.

In battle after battle, Lee managed to outthink and outmaneuver the Union armies, even though his forces were often outnumbered two to one. Even when the Army of Northern Virginia lost a battle, Lee's great dignity inspired his men and earned the respect of his enemies.

But Lee's army began to run short of men and supplies. When he tried to carry the war into the North, he suffered a devastating defeat at the Battle of Gettysburg (July 1-3, 1863). From that time on, Lee steadily retreated toward Richmond, Virginia. Finally, on April 9, 1865, he surrendered to Union General Ulysses S. Grant at Appomattox Court House. Although fighting continued elsewhere for a few weeks, the Civil War was over.

A dead Confederate soldier.

Lee surrenders at Appomattox Court House.

ACCEPTING DEFEAT

After the war, Lee urged Southerners to accept defeat with dignity and to work to restore the nation's unity. However, his own applications to the government for a pardon were never answered.

A FINAL HONOR

In September, 1865, Lee became president of Washington College in Lexington, Virginia. After his death, the name of the college was changed to Washington and Lee University.

UPDATE

The stately mansion owned by General and Mrs. Lee stood on the banks of the Potomac River, across from Washington, D.C. As soon as the Civil War began, federal troops seized the mansion, and the Lees never returned to it. It is now part of Arlington National Cemetery.

ULYSSES S. GRANT

CIVIL WAR GENERAL AND U.S. PRESIDENT

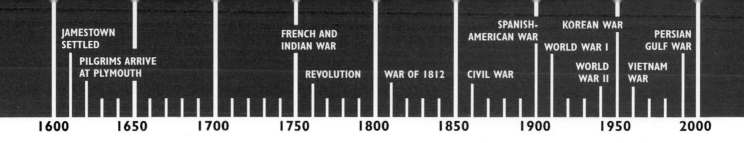

JAMESTOWN SETTLED

PILGRIMS ARRIVE AT PLYMOUTH

FRENCH AND INDIAN WAR

REVOLUTION

WAR OF 1812

CIVIL WAR

SPANISH-AMERICAN WAR

KOREAN WAR

WORLD WAR I

WORLD WAR II

VIETNAM WAR

PERSIAN GULF WAR

1600   1650   1700   1750   1800   1850   1900   1950   2000

- **Born on April 27, 1822, in Point Pleasant, Ohio**
- **Decorated for bravery in the Mexican War**
- **Served two terms as president (1868-1876)**
- **Died on July 23, 1885, in the Adirondack Mountains of New York**

Ulysses S. Grant was the exact opposite of Robert E. Lee. Where Lee was quiet and gentlemanly, Grant was rough and unpolished. Lee won battles for the South by brilliant maneuvering; Grant won battles for the North by hammering away at his enemy without mercy.

Grant was an unknown Union officer until 1862, when he led a Union attack on a Confederate fort in the Mississippi River Valley. It was the North's first victory of the war. In the months that followed, Grant scored more triumphs, winning control of the Mississippi and dividing the Confederacy in two.

President Abraham Lincoln now saw that Grant was the general he was looking for—a leader who could take on Lee. Grant was given command of all Union armies. With more soldiers and supplies, Grant's forces slowly wore down the Confederates, finally forcing Lee's surrender on April 9, 1865. Three years later, as the North's greatest hero, Grant was elected president.

General Grant and his men on the front lines.

Grant is sworn in as president.

AN ACCIDENTAL NAME CHANGE

Grant's real name was Hiram Ulysses Grant. He wanted to reverse the first two names because he didn't like the initials H.U.G. But when he entered West Point, he found that his name was mistakenly listed as Ulysses S. Grant. He decided to keep that name. In later years, he insisted that the S. did not stand for anything.

A TITLE OF HONOR

In 1866, Grant was given the title of general of the army. The only other person to be given that rank by Congress was George Washington in 1799.

PAYING DEBTS

After his two terms as president, Grant ran into financial problems when business associates defrauded him. To pay his debts, Grant spent the last years of his life writing the *Personal Memoirs of U.S. Grant*. The two volumes were published after his death and are considered one of the best-written histories of the Civil War.

CLARA BARTON

CIVIL WAR NURSE AND FOUNDER OF THE AMERICAN RED CROSS

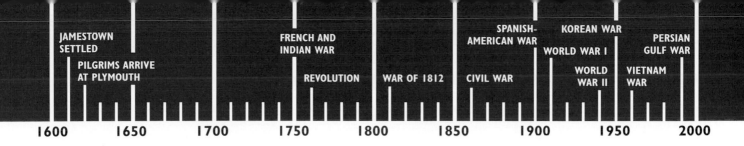

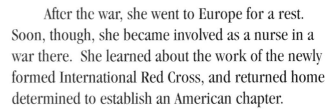

- **Born on December 25, 1821, in Oxford, Massachusetts**
- **Distributed medical supplies to Civil War battlefields**
- **Founded the American Red Cross**
- **Died on April 12, 1912, in Glen Echo, Maryland**

When the Civil War began, Clara Barton was working as a clerk in the U.S. Patent Office. She learned that the Union Army was short of medical supplies, so she immediately set up an agency to fill the need. Although she was told the battlefield was no place for a woman, she gained permission to go to the front lines. At one battle after another, she distributed supplies, nursed the wounded, and searched for men listed as missing. To the soldiers, she became known as "the angel of the battlefield."

A Union field hospital in Virginia in 1862.

After the war, she went to Europe for a rest. Soon, though, she became involved as a nurse in a war there. She learned about the work of the newly formed International Red Cross, and returned home determined to establish an American chapter.

After a ten-year struggle, the American National Red Cross was established in 1881, with Barton as its first president. She also wrote the American Amendment to the Geneva Convention, which was an international agreement that gave the Red Cross the authority to provide help in time of any disaster, such as floods or earthquakes, rather than only in wartime.

CLARA BARTON'S EARLY CAREER

For the first 18 years of her career, Clara Barton was a teacher. She opened a free school in New Jersey that became so successful that town leaders decided a woman should not be running it. Rather than serve a male principal, Barton resigned.

INDEPENDENT

Barton caused criticism of the Red Cross when she appeared on the battlefield in Cuba during the Spanish-American War (1898). Some people said that she should not have been there—she was 77 years old! Her insistence on doing things her way led to the request that she step down as American Red Cross president in 1904.

Heroes of the West

From the colonial period on, Americans looked westward. There always seemed to be new land and new opportunity over the next mountain or across the next river. Throughout the 1800s, the frontier was steadily pushed west. In the 1840s, many pioneers traveled across the Great Plains and the Rocky Mountains to reach California and Oregon. Then, after the Civil War, the Great Plains and mountain regions were rapidly filled in by settlers from the East.

A poster advertising Buffalo Bill's Wild West show.

The advance scouts of the westward movement were the mountain men—hunters and trappers who roamed the wilderness, often living with Native Americans. The Native Americans were friendly at first. But as wave after wave of white settlers arrived, they began to fight for their lands. From 1850 to 1890, war was almost constant between the Indians and the U.S. Army, sent to protect the frontier settlements. As in the Civil War, there were many courageous men and women on both sides of this long struggle.

This was also the time of the "Wild West." For a few short years, bands of cowboys led their herds on long cattle drives to towns on the railroad lines. These cow towns became notorious for their lawlessness. But the invention of barbed wire in 1876 led to the fencing-in of large areas of open range. By 1890, the Indian Wars were over, and the frontier was largely settled.

While the West was being settled, the United States was rapidly becoming a modern nation. Between 1850 and 1900, its population tripled to more than 75 million. Small towns grew into large cities. New inventions—electric lights, telephones, motion pictures, and automobiles—dramatically changed the way people lived.

1820 Jim Beckwourth goes west and becomes a mountain man

1840s Kit Carson serves as a guide for John Frémont

1847 Kit Carson escapes a Mexican force to get help for U.S. troops

1850 Jim Beckwourth blazes a trail from Nevada to California

1850s Kit Carson serves as an agent to the Ute Indians

1856 *The Life and Adventures of James P. Beckwourth* is published

1850–1890 Native Americans fight with the U. S. Army over new settlements

1861 The Civil War begins

1864 Kit Carson leads the Navajos on the Long Walk

1865 The Civil War ends

1869 Wild Bill Hickok becomes sheriff of Hays City, Kansas

1875 Annie Oakley wins a shooting contest

1877 Chief Joseph leads a group of Nez Percé across rugged terrain to escape U. S. troops

JIM BECKWOURTH

MOUNTAIN MAN AND SCOUT

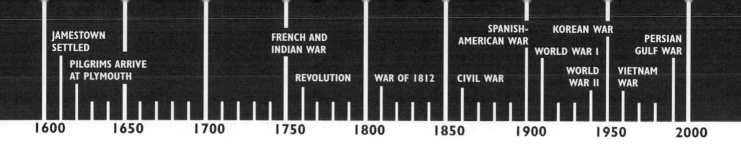

JAMESTOWN SETTLED		FRENCH AND INDIAN WAR			SPANISH-AMERICAN WAR	KOREAN WAR	PERSIAN GULF WAR
PILGRIMS ARRIVE AT PLYMOUTH						WORLD WAR I	
			REVOLUTION	WAR OF 1812	CIVIL WAR	WORLD WAR II	VIETNAM WAR

| 1600 | 1650 | 1700 | 1750 | 1800 | 1850 | 1900 | 1950 | 2000 |

• Born a slave on April 26, 1798, in Virginia

• Became a chief of the Crow nation

• Discovered a pass through the Sierra Nevada Mountains in California

• Died in 1867 or 1868 near Denver, Colorado Territory

Many African Americans escaped slavery and began new lives in the West as mountain men or cowboys. Jim Beckwourth was one of the most famous. His mother was a black slave; his father, Sir Jennings Beckwith, was white. Beckwith moved the family to Louisiana Territory and had Jim officially declared a free man.

Taking the name Beckwourth, Jim headed west in about 1820 and joined the mountain men in their endless search for furs and new lands. They explored every valley, stream, and mountain ridge, always far in advance of the settlers. For about six years, Beckwourth lived with the Crow Indians. He married a Crow woman and was made a chief before returning to white settlements.

Like other mountain men, Beckwourth served as a guide to wagon trains. In 1850, he blazed a trail from Nevada to California's Sacramento Valley. Thousands of settlers followed Beckwourth Pass in the Sierra Nevada to reach California. Today, a railroad runs through the pass that bears his name.

THE BECKWOURTH LEGEND

Famed for his strength and courage, Jim Beckwourth loved to tell tales about his exploits. He often was carried away by his own stories. In 1856, he published his autobiography, *The Life and Adventures of James P. Beckwourth*. While the book spread his fame, its stories are more legend than fact.

A MYSTERIOUS END

Beckwourth's death is as mysterious as the story of his life. According to some accounts, he was on a trip to visit the Crow when he was either killed in a hunting accident or poisoned by a jealous woman. Even the year of this death is unclear.

Pioneering settlers heading west.

KIT CARSON

MOUNTAIN MAN, GUIDE, AND SOLDIER

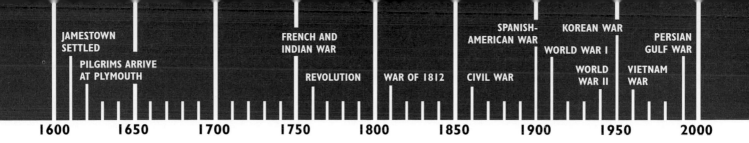

JAMESTOWN
SETTLED

PILGRIMS ARRIVE
AT PLYMOUTH

FRENCH AND
INDIAN WAR

REVOLUTION

WAR OF 1812

SPANISH-
AMERICAN WAR

CIVIL WAR

KOREAN WAR

WORLD WAR I

WORLD
WAR II

PERSIAN
GULF WAR

VIETNAM
WAR

1600   1650   1700   1750   1800   1850   1900   1950   2000

- Born December 24, 1809, in Madison County, Kentucky
- Served as a guide for the explorer John C. Frémont
- Became a hero of the Mexican War
- Died on May 23, 1868, at Fort Lyon, Colorado Territory

Few men on the American frontier were more admired and respected than Christopher ("Kit") Carson. Quiet and modest, he began his career as a mountain man when he was 20, hunting and trapping through much of the West. In the 1840s, he served as a guide for John C. Frémont, a famous explorer, in the Rocky Mountains, California, and Oregon.

Explorer John Frémont, who was guided by Kit Carson during the 1840s.

Carson joined Frémont in the fight to take California during the Mexican War. In 1847, he was sent from California to Washington, D.C., with news of the American victory. On the way, he was stopped by General Stephen W. Kearny, who ordered him to turn around and guide his troops to California. When Kearny's force was pinned down by Mexicans, Carson sneaked through enemy lines and walked 30 miles to get help. Then he delivered his messages to Washington—still in an amazingly short time. Overnight, Kit Carson became a national hero.

THE LONG WALK

As a colonel in the army, Carson spent most of the Civil War years fighting Apache and Navajo tribes. One event that he was not proud of took place in 1864, when he was ordered to move the Navajos from Canyon de Chelly to an army-controlled area. The Navajos today still call this 300-mile forced march the Long Walk. More than 200 Navajos died on the cruel journey.

INDIAN AGENT

Carson was admired for his work as agent to the Ute tribe in the 1850s. After the Civil War, though his health was failing, he traveled to Washington, D.C., with members of the tribe to present their case for land to the U.S. government.

UPDATE

Carson City, the capital of Nevada, is named after Kit Carson. Fort Carson in Colorado and the Carson River and Carson Pass in California are also named after the great frontiersman.

WILD BILL HICKOK

FAMED FRONTIER LAWMAN

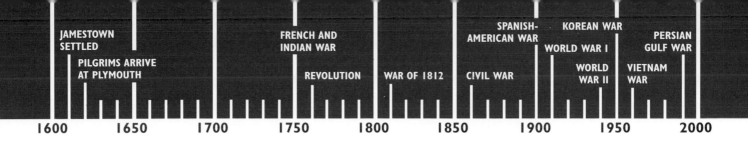

JAMESTOWN SETTLED

PILGRIMS ARRIVE AT PLYMOUTH

FRENCH AND INDIAN WAR

REVOLUTION

WAR OF 1812

SPANISH-AMERICAN WAR

CIVIL WAR

KOREAN WAR

WORLD WAR I

WORLD WAR II

VIETNAM WAR

PERSIAN GULF WAR

1600   1650   1700   1750   1800   1850   1900   1950   2000

- **Born on May 27, 1837, in Troy Grove, Illinois**
- **Served as a Union scout and spy in the Civil War**
- **Gained fame as a sheriff and marshal**
- **Killed during a card game on August 2, 1876, in Deadwood, Dakota Territory**

By the time he was 20, James Butler ("Wild Bill") Hickok was known as the greatest marksman on the frontier. After working as a stagecoach driver on the Oregon Trail, he became a scout and spy for the Union Army during the Civil War. Several times he was captured and sentenced to hang, but each time he managed to escape.

When he became sheriff of the wild cow town of Hays City, Kansas, in 1869, he was already famous for his courage and his skill with a gun. He managed to end the lawlessness in Hays City; he then did the same as the powerful marshal of Abilene, Kansas. Almost singlehandedly, he had tamed two of the Wild West's wildest towns.

Hickok toured for two years with Buffalo Bill's Wild West Show. He was married in 1876 but could not settle down. He moved on to the Dakota Territory, where he was shot dead in a saloon in the town of Deadwood.

THE BEGINNING OF THE LEGEND

While camping near his stagecoach on the Oregon Trail, Hickok was attacked by a bear. Badly mauled, and armed only with a knife, he managed to kill the wild beast. A few months later, while still recovering from his wounds, he was trapped by a gang of outlaws. Or perhaps he argued with the men—stories differ. In any case, he shot his way out, killing three of the outlaws. The two "episodes" made him a legendary figure. The legends about him continued to grow long after his death.

PEACE IN ABILENE

As marshal of Abilene, Wild Bill Hickok never had to draw his gun. By this time, his reputation was so great that no one dared to stir up trouble. He sometimes gave demonstrations of his fast draw and marksmanship, in case anyone had any doubts.

UPDATE

Hickok was shot in the back by a stranger during a poker game. The hand he was holding—aces and eights—is still known as the "dead man's hand."

Animals were pursued for entertainment during wild west shows.

CHIEF JOSEPH

CHIEF OF THE NEZ PERCÉ

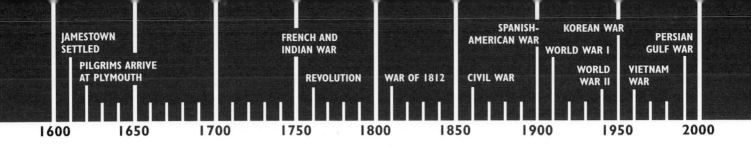

JAMESTOWN SETTLED

PILGRIMS ARRIVE AT PLYMOUTH

FRENCH AND INDIAN WAR

REVOLUTION

WAR OF 1812

SPANISH-AMERICAN WAR

CIVIL WAR

KOREAN WAR

WORLD WAR I

WORLD WAR II

VIETNAM WAR

PERSIAN GULF WAR

1600   1650   1700   1750   1800   1850   1900   1950   2000

- Born about 1840 in Wallowa Valley, Oregon
- Led the Nez Percé march to escape the U.S. Army
- Heroism created sympathy for the Native American cause
- Died on September 21, 1904, on the Colville Reservation, Washington

In 1877, Chief Joseph led a group of Nez Percé on one of the most amazing and heroic marches in American history.

Fighting between the Nez Percé and the U.S. Army began after Joseph and other chiefs refused to give up the tribe's lands in Oregon and move to a reservation in Idaho. Joseph won more than a dozen battles. But he was outnumbered and outgunned, and he knew that defeat would come. Instead of being forced onto a reservation, he decided to flee to Canada.

The incredible march of the Nez Percé began in the summer of 1877. Week after week, the group of about 750 men, women, and children managed to elude the U.S. Army. The desperate flight took the

Nez Percé through rugged terrain from Oregon through parts of Idaho, Wyoming, and Montana. Chief Joseph won respect for the brilliance with which he led the retreat and for his kindness, even to prisoners.

After traveling nearly 1,500 miles, the exhausted band stopped to rest on September 10. A fresh army division caught up and forced their surrender on October 5. The Nez Percé were less than 40 miles from Canada.

THE WORDS OF CHIEF JOSEPH

When Chief Joseph surrendered, his words were carefully written down by an army officer. The speech is one of the most famous in Native American history. Joseph ended by saying, "Hear me, my chiefs! I am tired; my heart is sick and sad. From where the sun now stands, I will fight no more forever."

CHIEF JOSEPH'S NAME

Chief Joseph's Nez Percé name, Hinmaton Yalaktit, means "Thunder Rolling in the Heights."

SENT TO OKLAHOMA

The army officer who accepted Joseph's surrender promised that the Nez Percé would be returned to their homes. Instead, they were sent to a reservation in Oklahoma. Many soon died there.

Members of the Nez Percé tribe pose for a photo in 1891.

ANNIE OAKLEY

SHARPSHOOTER AND PERFORMER

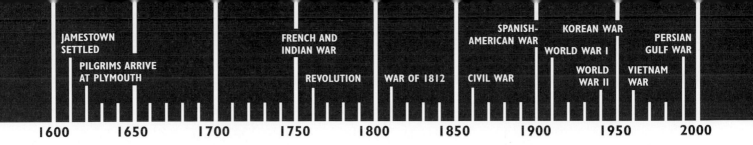

JAMESTOWN SETTLED

PILGRIMS ARRIVE AT PLYMOUTH

FRENCH AND INDIAN WAR

REVOLUTION

WAR OF 1812

SPANISH-AMERICAN WAR

KOREAN WAR

WORLD WAR I

PERSIAN GULF WAR

CIVIL WAR

WORLD WAR II

VIETNAM WAR

1600   1650   1700   1750   1800   1850   1900   1950   2000

- **Born August 13, 1860, in Darke County, Ohio**
- **Became the world's most famous sharpshooter**
- **Died on November 2, 1926, in Greenville, Ohio**

Annie Oakley never lived on the frontier, but her name has always been associated with the Wild West. That is because she was the star of Buffalo Bill's Wild West show. This show was one way that people in the East and Europe learned about the West. Oakley was also the best shot with a rifle anyone had ever seen.

When she was 15, Phoebe Anne Oakley Mozee won a shooting contest against a famous marksman named Frank Butler. A few years later, the two were married and began touring with Buffalo Bill. She became the star of the show as Miss Annie Oakley. The great Sioux chief, Sitting Bull, gave her the nickname Little Sure Shot.

Sitting Bull.

For years, Annie Oakley amazed audiences with her deadly aim. At a distance of 30 paces, she could split a playing card held on edge, puncture dimes tossed in the air, and extinguish a cigarette held in Butler's lips. To people throughout the world, Annie Oakley came to symbolize the spirit, independence, and skill of women on the frontier.

CHILDHOOD FAME

Oakley was becoming famous even before she bested Frank Butler. Her sharpshooting made her an outstanding hunter, and she was able to pay off the mortgage on her family's farm by selling game to city restaurants.

SMALL BUT TOUGH

Not quite five feet tall, Oakley was known for her toughness. In 1901, a train wreck left her partially paralyzed, and her career seemed to be over. But through endless hours of training, she restored her shooting skills. She was still astounding audiences in her sixties.

UPDATE

In 1946, Irving Berlin used Oakley's legendary life as the basis for his musical *Annie Get Your Gun*, which was later made into a movie.

The Early Twentieth Century

The Wright brothers fly their plane on December 17, 1903.

Between 1900 and 1950, the American people faced new challenges and new opportunities. Bustling cities were a sign of progress, but they also led to problems, such as poverty, slums, and crime. Courageous individuals did what they could to improve conditions. Gradually, Americans also turned to government for help with these problems.

While Americans no longer had a western frontier to settle, they found new areas to explore—frontiers in science and medicine, in air travel, and remote regions of the planet. The years 1900 to 1950 saw amazing advances in science and technology. Radio broadcasting began in the 1920s, and telephone service spanned oceans and continents. The Wright brothers made the first airplane flight in 1903; from that time on, brave men and women began pushing the boundaries of distance and speed. Modern transportation and communication brought all the world's nations into closer contact. This meant that an event in one part of the world would affect all other parts. At the same time, the United States emerged as one of the most powerful nations in the world. In 1917, the United States became involved in World War I (1914-1918), which had begun in Europe. Two decades later, the aggressions of Adolf Hitler, Nazi Germany, and Japan plunged the world into World War II (1939-1945). In both wars, thousands of Americans performed acts of heroism; only a few became famous.

C H R O N O L O G Y

1903 Mother Jones leads the March of the Mill Children

1909 Robert Peary and Matthew Henson become the first explorers to reach the North Pole

1912 Jim Thorpe wins two gold medals at the Stockholm Olympics

1917 America enters World War I

1918 Germany agrees to a truce in World War I

1927 Charles Lindbergh completes the first nonstop flight across the Atlantic

1931 Jane Addams wins the Nobel Peace Prize

1941 America enters World War II

1944 General Douglas MacArthur leads the U.S. in a major World War II victory in the Philippines

1945 Audie Murphy becomes a hero of World War II

1945 World War II ends

1947 Jackie Robinson becomes the first African American to play professional baseball and is named Rookie of the Year

1950 Jim Thorpe is named the greatest American athlete of the first half of the twentieth century

1950 The Korean War begins

1950 General Douglas MacArthur is named Supreme Commander of the United Nations force

JOHN J. PERSHING

COMMANDER OF AMERICAN FORCES IN WORLD WAR I

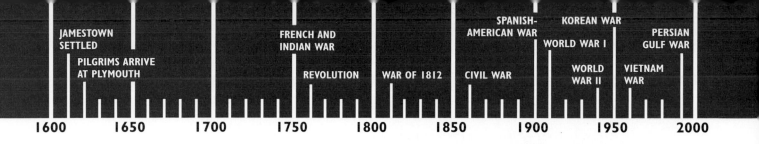

JAMESTOWN SETTLED		FRENCH AND INDIAN WAR		SPANISH-AMERICAN WAR	KOREAN WAR	PERSIAN GULF WAR	
PILGRIMS ARRIVE AT PLYMOUTH		REVOLUTION	WAR OF 1812	CIVIL WAR	WORLD WAR I WORLD WAR II	WORLD WAR I VIETNAM WAR	

1600   1650   1700   1750   1800   1850   1900   1950   2000

- Born on September 13, 1860, near Laclede, Missouri
- Decorated for bravery in the Spanish-American War, 1898
- Led American forces in World War I
- Died on July 15, 1948, in Washington, D.C.

When the United States entered World War I in 1917, the fighting had already been raging for nearly three years. America's allies—Britain and France—were exhausted by the deadly trench warfare against Germany, with most of the fighting on French soil. They hoped to use the fresh American troops as replacements for their tattered divisions.

But Major General John J. Pershing had different ideas. As commander of American forces in Europe, he insisted that U.S. troops fight in their own units, under their own flag. By the spring of 1918, Pershing's divisions were allowed to take the offensive. From September to November, more than 1 million Americans took part in a series of battles in the Meuse River valley. It was the largest American battle force up to that time. With Pershing's tactics and leadership, Americans broke through the enemy defenses, and Germany agreed to a truce on November 11, 1918. Pershing received a hero's welcome on his return home as the most famous American soldier of the war.

An American gun crew fights advancing Germans in 1918.

Yeomanettes—women attached to the U.S. Naval Reserve during World War I.

TRAINING SOLDIERS

Pershing had to create America's World War I army—the American Expeditionary Force—from scratch. Raw recruits were trained aboard ships on the way to France. At first there were not enough rifles, and some soldiers drilled with broomsticks instead.

A NEW RANK

After World War I, Pershing was named General of the Armies. He was the first person in American history to hold that title.

A PULITZER PRIZE

In 1931, Pershing wrote his memoirs, *My Experiences in the World War*. The book won a Pulitzer Prize and is considered an outstanding history of America's role in the war.

JANE ADDAMS

SOCIAL REFORMER AND PEACE ADVOCATE

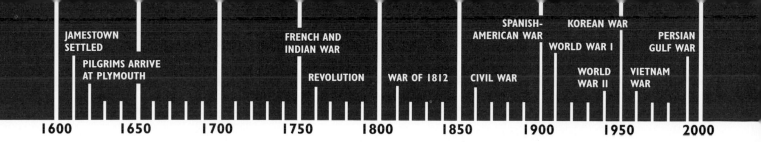

| JAMESTOWN SETTLED | | FRENCH AND INDIAN WAR | | | SPANISH-AMERICAN WAR | KOREAN WAR | |
| | PILGRIMS ARRIVE AT PLYMOUTH | | REVOLUTION | WAR OF 1812 | CIVIL WAR | WORLD WAR I | WORLD WAR II | PERSIAN GULF WAR | VIETNAM WAR |

1600 1650 1700 1750 1800 1850 1900 1950 2000

- **Born on September 5, 1860, in present-day Cedarville, Illinois**
- **Established Hull House, the nation's first settlement house**
- **A leader of the movement for women's right to vote**
- **Awarded the Nobel Peace Prize, 1931**
- **Died on May 21, 1935, in Chicago, Illinois**

Jane Addams was horrified by the conditions she saw in the slums of the nation's cities. In her day, there were no government agencies to help newcomers to the cities—immigrants from other countries and African Americans moving from the rural South. Many lived in deep poverty. Addams decided that she had to do something to help those less fortunate.

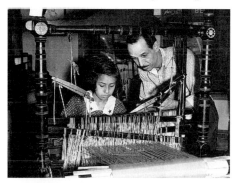

A young girl learns a skill at Hull House.

In 1889, Addams and a friend, Ellen Gates Starr, established Hull House in a Chicago slum. Hull House was the nation's first settlement house, a place where people could come to receive help and to learn new skills. In time, Hull House grew to include several buildings, a playground, and a summer camp in Wisconsin. The buildings included a health clinic, a gymnasium, a community kitchen, a day nursery, dormitories for single working women, and classrooms for learning art, music, crafts, and job-related skills. Hull House became famous throughout the world for its services, and settlement houses were established in 50 other cities. Addams provided much of the income needed to run Hull House by writing books.

Hull House.

CAMPAIGNING FOR REFORM

Jane Addams believed that poverty could be ended only by removing its root causes. She worked to improve factory and housing conditions. She also campaigned for voting rights for women and helped establish the first juvenile court system.

WORKING FOR WORLD PEACE

The suffering and destruction of World War I led Addams to the cause of international peace. She helped organize the Women's International League for Peace and Freedom and served as its first president. In 1931, she was co-winner of the Nobel Peace Prize.

UPDATE

By the 1960s, many Hull House activities had been taken over by government programs. In 1963, the University of Chicago wanted to expand its campus, so the Hull House Association moved its city headquarters to make room. Most of the original Hull House buildings were torn down, but the main house remains as a monument to its founder.

ROBERT PEARY

ARCTIC EXPLORER AND NAVAL OFFICER

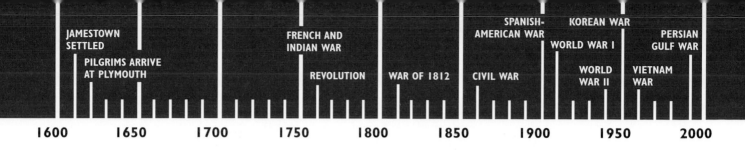

| JAMESTOWN SETTLED | | FRENCH AND INDIAN WAR | | | SPANISH-AMERICAN WAR | KOREAN WAR | PERSIAN GULF WAR |
| PILGRIMS ARRIVE AT PLYMOUTH | | REVOLUTION | WAR OF 1812 | CIVIL WAR | WORLD WAR I | WORLD WAR II / VIETNAM WAR | |

1600   1650   1700   1750   1800   1850   1900   1950   2000

- **Born on May 6, 1856, in Cresson, Pennsylvania**
- **Explored Greenland and the Arctic**
- **Led the first expedition to the North Pole**
- **Died on February 20, 1920, in Washington, D.C.**

From childhood, Robert Edwin Peary dreamed of exploring the mysterious, ice-filled Arctic regions. He became an officer in the U.S. Navy and used special leaves from duty to launch his explorations, beginning in 1881. On every expedition, he was accompanied by Matthew Henson, an African American who shared Peary's great courage and fascination for discovery.

Matthew Henson shows the Arctic regions he and Peary explored.

Between 1881 and 1896, Peary and Henson explored Greenland, finding evidence to prove it was an island. On one trip, they traveled 1,300 miles by dog sled. In 1898, they began searching for a route to the North Pole. Their first effort failed. In 1905, they set out again in the *Roosevelt*, a ship designed to sail through ice floes. Bad weather and thick ice forced them to turn back. They tried again in 1908, this time traveling over the ice by dog sled from Ellesmere Island.

On April 6, 1909, they finally reached their goal. Peary and Henson returned to a hero's welcome. Since Peary had planned, financed, and led the expeditions, his fame outshined Henson's, and the Navy promoted him to rear admiral. But he always insisted that he could not have succeeded without the expert guiding skills of Matthew Henson.

EVIDENCE FOR SCIENCE

On each of the Arctic expeditions, Peary made careful maps and gathered evidence for scientific study. On two of the trips to Greenland, he hauled giant meteors to the United States for study. At the North Pole, he took soundings that showed that the ocean beneath the Pole was deep.

WHO WAS FIRST?

When Peary and Henson returned from the North Pole, they learned that a man named Frederick Cook claimed to have reached the Pole a year earlier. Peary was bitterly disappointed by the controversy that followed. After several years of debate, most experts agreed that Cook's claim was not valid.

UPDATE

In the 1980s, new doubts were cast on Peary's claim of being the first to reach the North Pole. Studies of his journals showed that he had made errors in navigation. Scholars now think he might have stopped 60 miles short of his goal.

MOTHER JONES

LABOR LEADER AND SOCIAL REFORMER

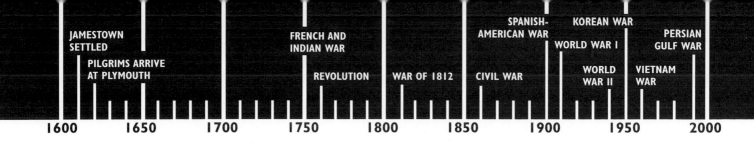

JAMESTOWN SETTLED

PILGRIMS ARRIVE AT PLYMOUTH

FRENCH AND INDIAN WAR

REVOLUTION

WAR OF 1812

CIVIL WAR

SPANISH-AMERICAN WAR

WORLD WAR I

KOREAN WAR

WORLD WAR II

VIETNAM WAR

PERSIAN GULF WAR

1600   1650   1700   1750   1800   1850   1900   1950   2000

- **Born on May 1, 1830, in Cork, Ireland**
- **Worked on behalf of miners for 50 years**
- **Led the March of the Mill Children**
- **Died on November 30, 1930, in Silver Spring, Maryland**

In her glasses, black bonnet, and dark clothes, Mary Harris ("Mother") Jones looked like a kindly grandmother. But to the men who worked the mines, and to their families, she was known as "the miner's angel." And the mine owners called her "the most dangerous woman in America." From the 1870s to the 1920s, Mother Jones was constantly on the scene of major strikes and labor conflicts all around the country, speaking out for the rights of workers and their families.

In spite of her gentle looks, Mother Jones could hold a crowd spellbound with her powerful speaking voice. Time after time, she showed remarkable courage, always urging peaceful methods, even when a strike had turned violent. One of her most successful campaigns was a children's march in 1903. She led 300 child workers from Pennsylvania mills on a week-long march to President Theodore Roosevelt's home in New York. The march created such strong sympathy for the children that 23 states passed strict laws against child labor.

PERSONAL TRAGEDY

Mother Jones experienced great tragedy in her private life. In 1867, while living in Tennessee, her husband and their four children died when a yellow-fever epidemic struck Memphis. She moved to Chicago, where, four years later, she lost all of her possessions in the Great Chicago Fire.

FACING DANGER

Stories of her courage helped make Mother Jones a legendary figure. On one occasion, for example, when a mine guard leveled his gun at her and threatened to shoot, she calmly walked up to him and placed her hand over the muzzle of the gun. She was jailed several times for leading strikes, but because of her age and courage, this only won sympathy for the strikers. In her nineties, she was still active in the coal mine regions. She died at age 100.

Young children work in a Georgia mill at the turn of the century.

JIM THORPE

STAR ATHLETE

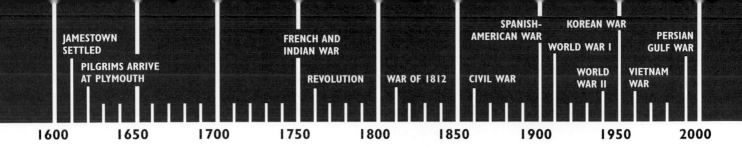

JAMESTOWN
SETTLED

PILGRIMS ARRIVE
AT PLYMOUTH

FRENCH AND
INDIAN WAR

REVOLUTION

WAR OF 1812

SPANISH-
AMERICAN WAR

KOREAN WAR

WORLD WAR I

PERSIAN
GULF WAR

WORLD
WAR II

VIETNAM
WAR

CIVIL WAR

1600   1650   1700   1750   1800   1850   1900   1950   2000

- Born on May 28, 1888, near Prague, Oklahoma
- Twice an All-American in football
- Winner of two gold medals in the 1912 Olympic Games
- Major league baseball player and professional football star
- Died on March 28, 1953, in Lomita, California

In 1911, tiny Carlisle Indian School in Pennsylvania became a powerhouse in college football. The main reason was a Native-American halfback named Jim Thorpe, one of the most amazing athletes in history. A powerful runner, an accurate kicker, and a terror on defense, Thorpe was named All-American in 1911 and 1912. In 1912, he scored 25 touchdowns and led Carlisle to a 27–6 win over Army.

Thorpe (back row, far right) and his famous football team from the Carlisle Indian School.

The year 1912 also witnessed Thorpe's greatest feat: At the Olympic Games in Stockholm, Sweden, he became the only man ever to win both the decathlon and pentathlon. But a year later, when Olympic officials learned that he had played minor-league baseball for two summers, his gold medals were taken from him for being a professional athlete.

Thorpe began playing major league baseball in 1913. He was also one of the first stars of

Thorpe as a professional baseball player.

professional football, playing from 1913 to 1928. In 1950, sports writers and broadcasters named him the greatest American athlete and the greatest football player of the first half of the century.

THORPE'S POPULARITY

Jim Thorpe was not only one of the greatest stars of professional football in its early years, but also one of the most popular. He was a coach as well as a player. And, in 1920–1921, he served as the first president of the association that later became the National Football League.

VERSATILITY

While Thorpe was playing professional football, he was also a major-league baseball player for seven years. Never a great star in baseball, he still managed to bat .327 for the Boston Braves in 1919, his last year. He was also outstanding in such sports as swimming, basketball, boxing, lacrosse, and hockey.

UPDATE

After years of effort by family and friends, Jim Thorpe's amateur status for 1912 was restored in 1973. Nine years later, the International Olympic Committee returned his two gold medals to his family and restored his name to the record books.

CHARLES A. LINDBERGH

AVIATION PIONEER

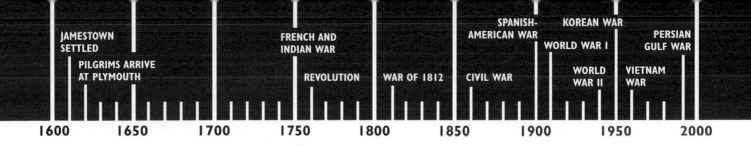

JAMESTOWN SETTLED		FRENCH AND INDIAN WAR			SPANISH-AMERICAN WAR	KOREAN WAR		PERSIAN GULF WAR
PILGRIMS ARRIVE AT PLYMOUTH		REVOLUTION	WAR OF 1812	CIVIL WAR	WORLD WAR I	WORLD WAR II	VIETNAM WAR	
1600	1650	1700	1750	1800	1850	1900	1950	2000

- **Born February 4, 1902, in Detroit, Michigan**
- **One of the first airmail pilots**
- **Gained fame for the first nonstop flight across the Atlantic**
- **Died on August 26, 1974, in Kipahulu, Maui, Hawaii**

On a dark, rainy morning in May 1927, a silver airplane called *The Spirit of St. Louis* struggled down the runway of a Long Island, New York, airfield. At the controls of the plane, which was heavily loaded with extra fuel, was a young pilot named Charles Augustus Lindbergh. He hoped to win a $25,000 prize for the first nonstop flight across the Atlantic Ocean from New York to Paris.

The headline announcing Lindbergh's success in 1927.

While millions waited to learn his fate, the plane droned over the Atlantic. Lindbergh found that his worst enemy was sleepiness. He had no radio. His only instrument was a compass. And yet 33 1/2 hours later, he landed safely outside Paris, as a crowd of 100,000 swarmed around the plane. Overnight, Lindbergh became known as the Lone Eagle—the world's most popular hero.

Lindbergh lost some of his popularity in 1940, when he opposed America's entry into World War II. But when the United States entered the war in 1941, he served as an aviation advisor and flew 50 combat missions. Several years later, he was named a brigadier general in the Air Force Reserve.

THE LINDBERGH KIDNAPPING

Lindbergh did not care for fame, and it brought him and his wife tragedy. In 1932, the Lindberghs' infant son was kidnapped and murdered. In a highly publicized trial, Bruno Hauptmann was convicted of the crime. The government then passed the "Lindbergh law," making kidnapping a federal crime.

FAMOUS AUTHORS

Both Charles Lindbergh and his wife, Anne Morrow Lindbergh, were outstanding writers. He won a Pulitzer Prize in 1953 for his autobiography, *The Spirit of St. Louis*. Her most famous book, *Gift From the Sea*, published in 1955, is still a best seller. She was a licensed pilot and often flew with her husband. Both Lindberghs were among the first Americans to urge the nation to protect natural resources.

DOUGLAS MACARTHUR

AMERICAN GENERAL IN WORLD WAR II

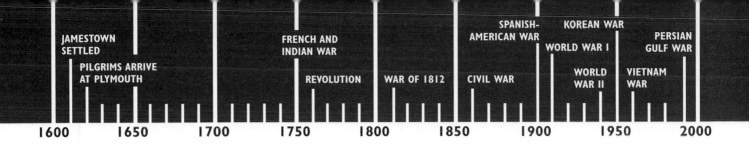

JAMESTOWN SETTLED		FRENCH AND INDIAN WAR		SPANISH-AMERICAN WAR	KOREAN WAR		PERSIAN GULF WAR
PILGRIMS ARRIVE AT PLYMOUTH					WORLD WAR I		
			REVOLUTION	WAR OF 1812	CIVIL WAR	WORLD WAR II	VIETNAM WAR

1600   1650   1700   1750   1800   1850   1900   1950   2000

- Born on January 26, 1880, near Little Rock, Arkansas
- Led Allied forces against Japan in World War II
- Supreme commander of U.N. forces in the Korean War (1950–1953)
- Died April 5, 1964, in Washington, D.C.

On December 7, 1941, Japanese forces attacked the U.S. naval base at Pearl Harbor, Hawaii, plunging the nation into World War II. On the same day, the Japanese also attacked the Philippines, where General Douglas MacArthur was stationed. As the Japanese forces gained control of the Philippines, MacArthur was ordered to escape to Australia and to begin planning a counter-offensive. As he left, the general vowed, "I shall return."

MacArthur kept his word. From his base in Australia, he commanded all Allied forces in the southwestern Pacific. Japan had conquered a huge empire in the Pacific and controlled countless islands. MacArthur designed a strategy of "island-hopping," which allowed him to recapture some islands while leap-frogging others that then became isolated from Japanese forces. In October 1944, after 30 months of tough island fighting, MacArthur waded ashore on the Philippines, victorious.

Italy's Mussolini, Japan's Tojo, and Germany's Hitler led the enemy Axis powers of World War II.

When the war ended in 1945, MacArthur was placed in command of the occupation of Japan. From 1945 to 1950, he performed his task brilliantly, helping to create a democratic government in Japan and restoring the nation's economy.

EARLY CAREER

In 1903, Douglas MacArthur graduated from West Point first in his class, with one of the highest scores ever achieved there. After being decorated many times for his service in World War I, he became superintendent of West Point (1919–1922) and, later, army chief of staff (1930-1933).

MACARTHUR AND THE PHILIPPINES

MacArthur resigned from the army in 1937 to spend four years helping the Philippines prepare for independence from the United States. Independence was achieved soon after the end of World War II.

THE GENERAL AND THE PRESIDENT

When Communist North Korea invaded South Korea in 1950, MacArthur was named supreme commander of the United Nations force fighting to preserve South Korea's independence. In 1951, however, MacArthur publicly criticized President Harry S. Truman for the way the war was being conducted. The president had no choice but to remove MacArthur from command.

AUDIE MURPHY

WORLD WAR II HERO AND ACTOR

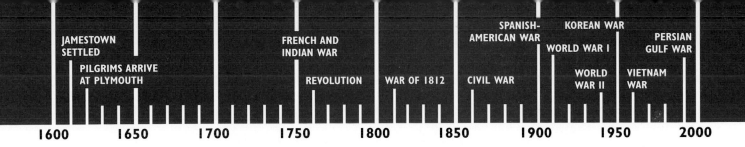

						SPANISH-AMERICAN WAR	KOREAN WAR	
JAMESTOWN SETTLED		FRENCH AND INDIAN WAR					WORLD WAR I	PERSIAN GULF WAR
PILGRIMS ARRIVE AT PLYMOUTH							WORLD WAR II	VIETNAM WAR
		REVOLUTION	WAR OF 1812	CIVIL WAR				

1600   1650   1700   1750   1800   1850   1900   1950   2000

- Born on June 20, 1924, in Hunt County, Texas
- Became the most decorated hero of World War II
- As an actor, appeared in nearly 40 films
- Died in a plane crash on May 28, 1971, near Roanoke, Virginia

World War II produced many American heroes, but perhaps none was more amazing than Audie Murphy. He enlisted in the army in 1942, just before his eighteenth birthday. He fought in the American campaigns waged in North Africa, Sicily, Italy, France, and Germany. He was wounded three times and decorated for bravery several times, rising in rank from private to lieutenant.

Audie Murphy on a movie set in 1959.

Murphy's most famous act of heroism came on January 26, 1945, in the closing weeks of the war. He was cut off from his unit and surrounded by a German force. Murphy leaped into a burning tank destroyer and trained its machine gun on the advancing Germans. In one of the greatest individual feats of the war, he single-handedly held off the German force of 6 tanks and 250 men. Soon after, he was awarded the Congressional Medal of Honor for this courageous act. He also received 25 other medals, making him World War II's most decorated and popular hero.

SHARING THE HONORS

Besides his American medal, Audie Murphy received the highest honors of both France and Belgium. Later, he gave away all the medals to the children of relatives. He explained, "I never felt that [the medals] entirely belonged to me. My whole unit earned them, but I didn't know how to give them to the whole unit."

AUTHOR AND ACTOR

In 1949, Audie Murphy wrote his war memoirs. The book—*To Hell and Back*—became a best seller. A movie based on the book starred Murphy playing himself. This launched him on a successful movie career.

JACKIE ROBINSON

FIRST AFRICAN AMERICAN IN MAJOR LEAGUE BASEBALL

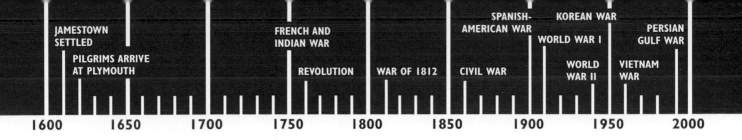

- **Born on January 31, 1919, in Cairo, Georgia**
- **Won honors as Rookie of the Year and Most Valuable Player**
- **Worked for racial equality**
- **Died on October 24, 1972, in Stamford, Connecticut**

April 11, 1947, was a historic day for major league baseball and for the entire nation. When the major-league baseball season opened that day, at second base for the Brooklyn Dodgers was Jack Roosevelt Robinson, the first African American to play baseball for a major league team.

Jackie Robinson faced a difficult challenge because some whites did not want African Americans in major league baseball or in other major team sports. At first, he was booed by rowdy fans and treated rudely by players on other teams. He also received dozens of threats on his life. In many cities, Robinson was not allowed in the same hotels or restaurants as his teammates.

Jackie Robinson slides as he steals home.

He handled the pressure with amazing calm, and people quickly realized that he was one of the most talented and exciting players in the game. Robinson was an outstanding hitter, fielder, and base stealer. He was named Rookie of the Year in 1947. Two years later, he won the batting championship and was named Most Valuable Player. He retired after the 1956 season with a lifetime batting average of .311, and he was elected to the Baseball Hall of Fame in 1962. Jackie Robinson's courageous example paved the way for the full integration of major-league baseball in the years that followed.

STEALING HOME

Whenever Jackie Robinson reached third base, a wave of excitement would sweep through the crowd. The reason: He was one of the few base stealers who could manage to steal home.

WORKING FOR EQUALITY

After he retired from baseball, Robinson became vice president of a major corporation and was also a special assistant on community relations for the governor of New York. In both these positions, he worked to improve racial relations and to open new job opportunities for members of minority groups. He also started the Jackie Robinson Foundation to help young people.

A MEDICAL DISCHARGE

Robinson served in the army in World War II (1941–1945) and received a medical discharge for what the army called "football ankles." The year of his discharge he played both professional baseball and football for African-American teams.

America Since 1950

Americans enjoyed a wave of prosperity in the years following World War II. Businesses expanded, new suburbs rapidly surrounded older cities, and downtown areas were renewed. With the tremendous output from its farms and factories, the United States was able to help rebuild the countries that had been devastated by war.

But the prosperity of postwar America was not shared equally. Millions of African Americans and other minorities found that the doors of opportunity were often closed to them. Nearly a century after slavery ended, African Americans found themselves living in segregated (separate) neighborhoods, with poor schools and few services. Courageous African Americans led the way in a new movement for civil rights. They were soon joined by members of other

Rock 'n' roll legend Elvis Presley.

minorities—men and women who took great risks to stand up for their rights. The age of space exploration provided Americans with bold new frontiers, and new heroes. The 1950s and 1960s saw the emergence of rock 'n' roll and the mega-stars it created. Among them: Chuck Berry, Elvis Presley, the Beatles, and Buddy Holly. In the 1960s, Americans became aware of still another new challenge: the need to protect the environment. From colonial times, Americans thought of their country as a land of endless resources. But modern industries have overused those resources and pumped numerous dangerous poisons into the air and water. Various organized efforts to preserve and protect the natural world have produced some of the heroes featured in the pages that follow.

C H R O N O L O G Y

1952 Dr. Jonas Salk announces the creation of a polio vaccine

1953 Dr. Salk announces the creation of an influenza vaccine

1953 The Korean War ends

1955 Rosa Parks refuses to sit in a blacks-only section of a public bus

1956 The Supreme Court declares racial segregation of public transportation unconstitutional

1962 Rachel Carson launches the U.S. environmental movement with her book *Silent Spring*

1963 Martin Luther King, Jr., leads the March on Washington and delivers his famous "I Have a Dream" speech

1963 Jacqueline Kennedy inspires the nation with her courage after her husband, John F. Kennedy, is assassinated

1964 Martin Luther King, Jr., is awarded the Nobel Peace Prize

1964 America becomes fully involved in the Vietnam War

1968 Cesar Chavez leads a national boycott against California grape growers

1969 Neil Armstrong becomes the first person to walk on the moon

1975 American involvement in Vietnam ends

1986 The birthday of Martin Luther King, Jr., becomes an official U.S. holiday

1991 General H. Norman Schwarzkopf commands Allied forces in the Persian Gulf War

JONAS SALK

PHYSICIAN AND MEDICAL RESEARCHER

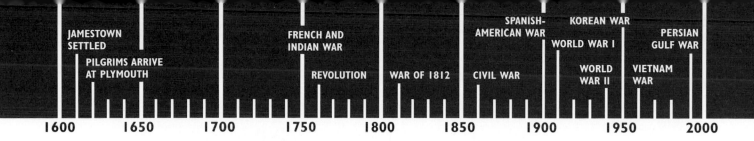

JAMESTOWN SETTLED

PILGRIMS ARRIVE AT PLYMOUTH

FRENCH AND INDIAN WAR

REVOLUTION

WAR OF 1812

CIVIL WAR

SPANISH-AMERICAN WAR

WORLD WAR I

KOREAN WAR

WORLD WAR II

VIETNAM WAR

PERSIAN GULF WAR

1600   1650   1700   1750   1800   1850   1900   1950   2000

- **Born on October 28, 1914, in New York City**
- **Developed the first polio vaccine**
- **Also developed vaccinations for influenza**
- **Has worked to find vaccines for cancer and for AIDS**
- **Died on June 23, 1995, in La Jolla, California**

In 1949, Dr. Jonas Salk set out to try to stop a deadly disease, one that had meant fear and sickness for millions of Americans in the 1930s and 1940s. The disease was infantile paralysis, or poliomyelitis—polio for short. There was no cure for polio, which is caused by a virus. The virus struck children more often than adults, killing some victims and leaving

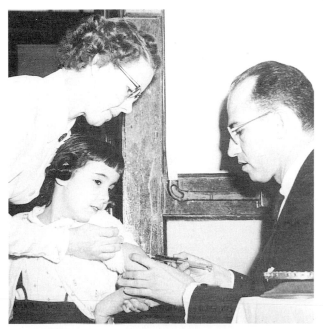

Dr. Salk vaccinates a young girl in 1956.

others seriously crippled. During severe epidemics, public playgrounds and swimming pools sometimes closed for months. Children often were not allowed to play with their friends. In 1952 alone there were more than 50,000 cases of polio in the United States and 3,300 deaths.

The March of Dimes Foundation had named Salk to head a three-year study of the polio virus. A year after the 1952 epidemic, Salk and his team announced success with an experimental polio vaccine. All across the nation, then the world, people lined up for their polio shots. With this triumph, the dreaded polio epidemics had come to an end.

In 1953, Salk was able to announce another successful vaccine. This one, to protect against influenza—the flu—had been the target of Salk's research since 1942. Today's flu shots have helped to make this killer disease far less dangerous.

A FAMOUS POLIO SURVIVOR

In 1921, Franklin D. Roosevelt was stricken with polio at the age of 38. Although he remained crippled for life, Roosevelt overcame his disability to become the nation's president from 1933 until his death in 1945. His leadership helped establish the March of Dimes Foundation.

THE SALK INSTITUTE

In 1963, Dr. Salk became the founder and director of the Salk Institute for Biological Studies in La Jolla, California. He has always refused to make personal profit from his research.

UPDATE

Through the early 1980s, Dr. Salk and his associates searched for vaccines to protect against certain kinds of cancer and, more recently, AIDS.

ROSA PARKS

CIVIL RIGHTS WORKER

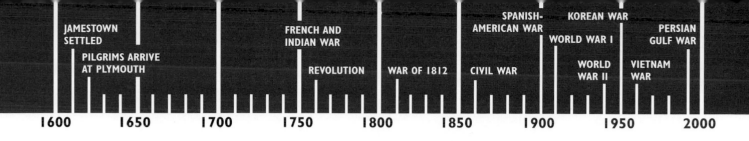

JAMESTOWN SETTLED		FRENCH AND INDIAN WAR			SPANISH-AMERICAN WAR	KOREAN WAR	
PILGRIMS ARRIVE AT PLYMOUTH						WORLD WAR I	PERSIAN GULF WAR
		REVOLUTION	WAR OF 1812	CIVIL WAR		WORLD WAR II	VIETNAM WAR

| 1600 | 1650 | 1700 | 1750 | 1800 | 1850 | 1900 | 1950 | 2000 |

- **Born September 11, 1912, in Tuskegee, Alabama**
- **Her action triggered the Montgomery bus boycott, a key event in the civil rights movement**
- **Became a symbol of peaceful resistance to racial segregation**

In Montgomery, Alabama, as in all areas of the South, African Americans were expected to obey the laws of segregation, to be separated from white people. On public buses, that meant taking a back seat—or no seat, if a white person entered and the bus was full. On December 1, 1955, a bus driver ordered a seamstress named Rosa Parks to give up her seat to a white man. When she refused, she was arrested and fined.

The matter might have stopped there. But Parks agreed to let the National Association for the Advancement of Colored People (NAACP) fight her case in court. They argued that segregated seats deprived Rosa Parks of her basic constitutional rights. At the same time, leaders asked Montgomery's African Americans to boycott, or refuse to ride, the city buses. Week after week, the buses were nearly empty, even though people were threatened by angry crowds of white segregationists. After 382 days, the boycott ended when the Supreme Court agreed that segregated seats were in fact unconstitutional. The idea of peaceful resistance to segregation rapidly spread throughout the South. Through her brave act, Parks helped launch the modern civil rights movement.

QUIET HEROES

The Montgomery bus boycott and other civil rights actions succeeded because thousands of African Americans were willing to risk danger by resisting the segregation laws. Like Parks, they did not want to be heroes; instead, they quietly stood up for their rights.

MOTHER OF A MOVEMENT

Rosa Parks lost her job because of her courageous action. That did not deter her, however. After the Montgomery bus boycott ended, she moved to Detroit, Michigan. She is sometimes called "the mother of the civil rights movement." Parks continued to work for civil rights for many years, but always stayed in the background.

President Clinton and Cicely Tyson greet Rosa Parks at a function held to honor her achievements in 1995.

91

MARTIN LUTHER KING, JR.

MINISTER AND CIVIL RIGHTS LEADER

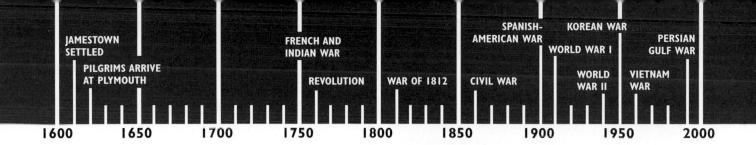

JAMESTOWN SETTLED		FRENCH AND INDIAN WAR			SPANISH-AMERICAN WAR	KOREAN WAR	PERSIAN GULF WAR
PILGRIMS ARRIVE AT PLYMOUTH					WORLD WAR I		
		REVOLUTION	WAR OF 1812	CIVIL WAR	WORLD WAR II	VIETNAM WAR	

| 1600 | 1650 | 1700 | 1750 | 1800 | 1850 | 1900 | 1950 | 2000 |

- **Born on January 15, 1929, in Atlanta, Georgia**
- **The most famous leader of the civil rights movement**
- **Led the March on Washington in 1963**
- **Awarded the Nobel Peace Prize in 1964**
- **Killed by an assassin on April 4, 1968, in Memphis, Tennessee**

The Reverend Martin Luther King, Jr., was the young pastor of a church in Montgomery, Alabama, when he was asked to lead the city bus boycott in 1955. African Americans and whites alike were impressed by his leadership and his eloquent speeches during the boycott.

The March on Washington.

For the next 12 years, King led the civil rights movement through some of it most dramatic moments. By organizing large peaceful protests, he helped create nationwide sympathy for African Americans in their demand for an end to racial segregation and discrimination. King taught a philosophy of nonviolence, even when protesters were met with violence. When King and other marchers were jailed or beaten, people throughout the world could see the evil of segregation. This forced the government to take action, and the walls of segregation began to crumble. King was killed by an assassin in 1968, but his words and his example continue to inspire people to this day.

Martin Luther King, Jr. delivers his "I Have a Dream" speech.

"I HAVE A DREAM"

In August 1963, King led more than 200,000 people in a march on Washington, D.C., to support a new civil rights law. From the steps of the Lincoln Memorial, he delivered his most famous speech. It included the words, "I have a dream that one day this nation will rise up and live out the true meaning of its creed: '... that all men are created equal.'"

THE COURAGE OF NONVIOLENT PROTEST

During the Montgomery bus boycott the Kings' home was fire-bombed. On other occasions, King and other civil rights advocates, or supporters, were beaten by mobs or thrown into jail. Through every test, King always held firmly to his belief in nonviolence. His courage, and that of all his followers, earned great respect for the civil rights cause.

UPDATE

In 1986, Martin Luther King, Jr.'s, birthday—January 15—was officially established by Congress as a federal holiday.

CESAR CHAVEZ

LABOR ORGANIZER AND CIVIL RIGHTS LEADER

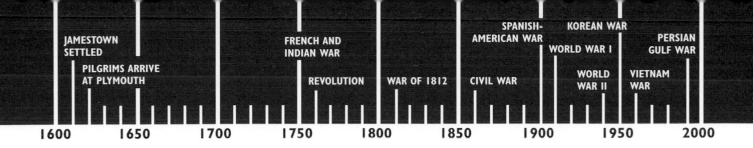

JAMESTOWN SETTLED

PILGRIMS ARRIVE AT PLYMOUTH

FRENCH AND INDIAN WAR

REVOLUTION

WAR OF 1812

SPANISH-AMERICAN WAR

CIVIL WAR

KOREAN WAR

WORLD WAR I

WORLD WAR II

VIETNAM WAR

PERSIAN GULF WAR

1600   1650   1700   1750   1800   1850   1900   1950   2000

- Born on March 31, 1927, near Yuma, Arizona
- Formed the first union for farm workers
- Gained respect for leading nonviolent protests
- Helped improve living and working conditions for American farm workers
- Died April 13, 1993, in San Luis, Arizona

As a boy growing up in Arizona and California, Cesar Estrada Chavez knew the hard life of a migrant farm worker. Most of the families, like his own, were newcomers from Mexico and Central America. They had to move often to be where crops were ready for harvest. The farm owners housed them in miserable migrant camps, paid very low wages, and treated them poorly.

Chavez devoted his life to improving conditions for the farm workers. He formed a union, the United Farm Workers of America (UFW). In 1968, he led a nationwide boycott against California grape owners, urging people not to buy grapes as a protest against unfair treatment of workers. Chavez also led strikes and peaceful marches to demand laws to protect the farm workers. His nonviolent methods and skill at organizing captured nationwide attention. The grape growers finally agreed to settle with the union, and growers of other crops slowly followed. Through 30 years of dedicated work, Cesar Chavez helped to improve wages and living conditions for farm workers in California, the Southwest, and Florida.

DRAMATIC ACTION

Chavez looked for ways to make the public aware of La Causa, which is Spanish for "The Cause" of the farm workers. One method he used was a hunger strike, or fast, which drew the attention of newspapers and television.

A SECOND BOYCOTT

In 1984, the grape growers refused the UFW's demand to control the use of pesticides on crops. Cesar Chavez again asked people throughout the nation to boycott (refuse to buy) California grapes. Few people thought the boycott would work. But millions of sympathetic people honored it, and the growers finally agreed to use fewer chemicals.

Cesar Chavez leads the United Farm Workers in a protest.

JACQUELINE KENNEDY ONASSIS

FIRST LADY

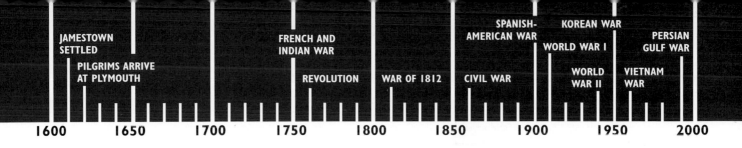

JAMESTOWN SETTLED
PILGRIMS ARRIVE AT PLYMOUTH
FRENCH AND INDIAN WAR
REVOLUTION
WAR OF 1812
CIVIL WAR
SPANISH-AMERICAN WAR
KOREAN WAR
WORLD WAR I
WORLD WAR II
PERSIAN GULF WAR
VIETNAM WAR

1600 1650 1700 1750 1800 1850 1900 1950 2000

- **Born on July 28, 1929, in Southampton, New York**
- **One of the most popular First Ladies in U.S. history**
- **Inspired the nation with her courage after the assassination of her husband**
- **Died on May 19, 1994, in New York City**

On November 22, 1963, President John F. Kennedy was shot by an assassin while riding in a motorcade in Dallas, Texas. At his side in the open limousine was his wife, Jacqueline Bouvier Kennedy. The tragedy of the assassination sent the entire nation and the world into shock.

Over the days and weeks of mourning that followed, Jacqueline Kennedy provided a shining example for Americans. The image of the president's widow, veiled and dressed in black, with her two young children at her side, is the one thing that most people remember from the funeral. Her calm strength and courage helped to pull the country through one of the worst episodes in its history.

Jacqueline Kennedy was already well-loved by the public. As First Lady, she had served as a goodwill ambassador by traveling to other countries. She had made the nation's capital a center of culture, inviting famous artists and performers to the White House. And her taste and style helped set the tone of the Kennedy presidency.

RESTORING THE WHITE HOUSE

When Jacqueline Kennedy became First Lady in January 1961, she was appalled at the run-down condition of the White House. She set to work on a major restoration of the president's home. To ensure that the work would be historically accurate, furnishings from past presidential administrations were purchased and moved to Washington. The return of the White House to its former elegance gave people new pride in this national landmark.

A NEW LIFE

After President Kennedy's death, Jacqueline Kennedy left Washington, hoping to escape the public spotlight. In 1968, she married Aristotle Onassis, a Greek shipowner, and moved to Greece. He died in 1975, and she moved to New York City, where she worked as a book editor. She cherished her privacy, but she was never able to completely avoid publicity.

First Lady Jacqueline Kennedy leads her son to the funeral of John F. Kennedy in 1963.

NEIL ARMSTRONG

ASTRONAUT AND TEST PILOT

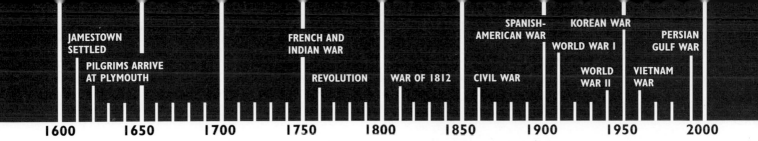

| JAMESTOWN SETTLED | | FRENCH AND INDIAN WAR | | | SPANISH-AMERICAN WAR | KOREAN WAR | | PERSIAN GULF WAR |
| PILGRIMS ARRIVE AT PLYMOUTH | | REVOLUTION | WAR OF 1812 | CIVIL WAR | WORLD WAR I | WORLD WAR II | VIETNAM WAR | |

1600   1650   1700   1750   1800   1850   1900   1950   2000

- Born on August 5, 1930, near Wapakoneta, Ohio
- A hero of the Korean War as a fighter pilot
- The first human to set foot on the moon

On July 20, 1969, millions of people around the world stared at their television sets and held their breath. On the screens, they saw a tiny craft pull away from the *Apollo 11*, a spacecraft hovering above the surface of the moon, half a million miles away. Inside the small module, named the *Eagle*, were astronauts Neil Alden Armstrong and Edwin ("Buzz") Aldrin, Jr. As the *Eagle* descended to the moon surface, the *Apollo 11* was kept in lunar orbit by a third astronaut, Michael Collins. The three men had left Earth on their historic mission on July 16.

As the *Eagle* settled softly on the lunar surface, relieved television viewers heard Armstrong say, "The

The first moon landing.

Eagle has landed!" Minutes later, Armstrong climbed down a ladder and became the first human to set foot on the moon. "That's one small step for a man," Armstrong declared, "and one giant leap for mankind!"

After ten years of effort in America's space program, the lunar landing represented one of the most dramatic moments in history. Armstrong, Aldrin, and Collins returned safely to Earth and were given a huge welcome from a grateful nation. Neil Armstrong, a quiet, modest man, with a boyish grin, became the greatest hero of space exploration.

Armstrong and fellow astronauts after splashing down in *Gemini 8*.

FIGHTER PILOT

As a young man, Armstrong was a navy fighter pilot in the Korean War (1950–1953). He flew 78 combat missions, was shot down but returned to action, and was awarded the Air Medal three times.

TEST PILOT

As a civilian test pilot, Armstrong set records for speed and altitude. Of all the experimental aircraft that he flew, his favorite was the *Bell X-15* rocket plane. The X-15 climbed to a record altitude of 67 miles. It reached a top speed of 4,534 miles per hour—twice as fast as a rifle bullet!

EMERGENCY EXPERIENCE

Armstrong became an astronaut in 1962. One reason he was chosen for the moon landing was the way that he handled a crisis during an earlier space flight. In the 1966 *Gemini 8* mission, he completed the first-ever docking of a spacecraft with a target vehicle. But both vehicles suddenly went into a wild spin. Armstrong coolly handled the emergency and returned safely to Earth.

RACHEL CARSON

WRITER, BIOLOGIST, AND ENVIRONMENTALIST

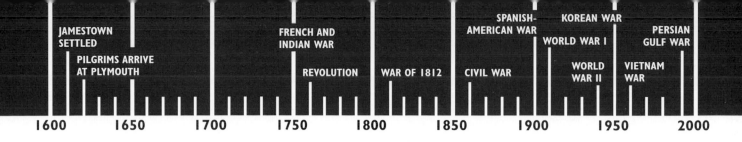

					SPANISH-	KOREAN WAR	
JAMESTOWN SETTLED			FRENCH AND INDIAN WAR		AMERICAN WAR	WORLD WAR I	PERSIAN GULF WAR
PILGRIMS ARRIVE AT PLYMOUTH			REVOLUTION	WAR OF 1812	CIVIL WAR	WORLD WAR II	VIETNAM WAR

1600   1650   1700   1750   1800   1850   1900   1950   2000

- **Born May 27, 1907, in Springdale, Pennsylvania**
- **Her book *Silent Spring* helped launch the environmental movement**
- **Died on April 14, 1964, in Silver Spring, Maryland**

Rachel Carson had no intention of being a hero or changing the course of history. Instead, she wanted to quietly pursue her two great interests: the study of nature, and writing. She became a biologist for the U.S. Fish and Wildlife Service, and wrote several best-selling books about the sea.

Her keen interest in nature led Carson to worry about the heavy use of chemicals in farming and industry. While chemicals like DDT were effective for killing pests, she saw that they were harming wildlife and upsetting nature's balance. In 1962, she wrote *Silent Spring*, describing the dangers she saw.

The book was a wake-up call for the American people. It has been called one of the most important books of the century. At first, Carson was criticized. Chemical manufacturers tried to paint her as a troublemaker and a crackpot. but through her

A plaque commemorates Rachel Carson's achievements at the Carson Wildlife Refuge in Maine.

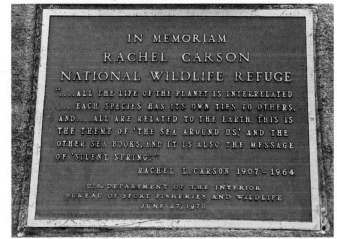

work, people all over the world became aware of the urgent need to protect the environment. During the years that followed the publication of her book, new environmental laws were passed and government agencies were set up to help. Almost singlehandedly, Rachel Carson had launched the nation on an environmental movement that still continues to this day.

A CHANGE IN COURSE

When she was a student, Rachel Carson hoped to become a writer. But an outstanding science teacher helped her to develop a love of studying nature. Then, during her summer studies at the Marine Biological Laboratory in Woods Hole, Massachusetts, she became fascinated by the sea. For many years, her major interest was studying life in the sea.

THE LIFE OF THE SEA

Before *Silent Spring*, Carson had written three other books: *Under the Sea Wind*, in 1941; *The Sea Around Us*, in 1951; *The Edge of the Sea*, in 1955. Her combination of scientific knowledge and a beautiful writing style made her famous. Like *Silent Spring*, *The Sea Around Us* remains a best-seller today and has been translated into more than 40 languages.

H. NORMAN SCHWARZKOPF

AMERICAN COMMANDER IN THE PERSIAN GULF WAR

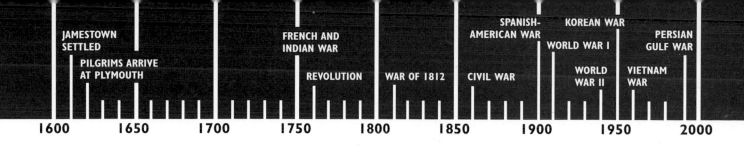

JAMESTOWN SETTLED

PILGRIMS ARRIVE AT PLYMOUTH

FRENCH AND INDIAN WAR

REVOLUTION

WAR OF 1812

CIVIL WAR

SPANISH-AMERICAN WAR

WORLD WAR I

KOREAN WAR

WORLD WAR II

VIETNAM WAR

PERSIAN GULF WAR

1600   1650   1700   1750   1800   1850   1900   1950   2000

- **Born on August 22, 1934, in Trenton, New Jersey**
- **Honored for bravery in the Vietnam War**
- **Commanded allied forces in the Persian Gulf War**

In the summer of 1990, General H. Norman Schwarzkopf, commander of U.S. forces in the Middle East, was developing a plan of action for a desert war. During his planning, Iraq invaded Kuwait, its neighbor on the Persian Gulf. Kuwait, a tiny country friendly to the United States, was of great strategic importance because of its enormous oil fields. Both the United States and the United Nations condemned the invasion and gave Iraq a deadline of January 15, 1991, to withdraw from Kuwait.

As the deadline approached, the first part of Schwarzkopf's plan, called "Desert Shield," was put into effect. A huge military force, representing 28 nations, was assembled in the Persian Gulf region. When the January 15 deadline passed with Iraq still in Kuwait, Desert Shield became "Desert Storm." Air attacks were launched against Iraq, cutting communications and supply lines and destroying bases and missile sites. Six weeks later, Schwarzkopf ordered ground troops into action. Many people had feared that a desert land war would cost the allies heavy casualties. But Schwarzkopf had planned well. In less than 100 hours, the coalition forces smashed through the enemy's defenses and Iraq quickly agreed to a cease-fire. The Persian Gulf War had ended in a stunning victory for American-led forces. "Stormin' Norman," as his troops called him, returned home to a hero's welcome. He retired from military service a few months later.

EARLY LIFE

Norman Schwarzkopf spent most of his teenage years in foreign countries. His father was an army general and then became head of the national police force in Iran. Later, at West Point, Schwarzkopf was on both the football and wrestling teams.

HEROISM IN VIETNAM

During the Vietnam War, Schwarzkopf served two tours of combat duty. His medals included three Silver Stars, three Bronze Stars, a Distinguished Service Medal, and two Purple Hearts. After that war was over, he promised himself that, if he ever commanded American forces in a war, he would do everything in his power to keep casualties low. He kept his promise in the Persian Gulf War. Only 148 Americans died in the fighting.

General Schwarzkopf is greeted by supporters in Florida.

You will find excellent biographies of many of the people in this book at your school or hometown library. Listed here are biography series that include books on some of those individuals:

Childhood of Famous Americans (Macmillan Publishing Company, 1991).
  Individual biographies of Molly Pitcher, Paul Revere, Robert E. Lee, Clara Barton, Annie Oakley, and Jim Thorpe.

Cornerstones of Freedom Series (Childrens Press).
  Includes books about Clara Barton, Robert Peary, and Apollo 11 *(Neil Armstrong).*

Discovery Biographies (Chelsea House, 1987-1991).
  Biographies of Daniel Boone, Dolley Madison, Andrew Jackson, Frederick Douglass, Robert E. Lee, Clara Barton, Jim Beckwourth, Charles Lindbergh, and Rachel Carson.

Easy Biographies (Troll 1986-1990).
  Includes books about Daniel Boone, Patrick Henry, John Paul Jones, Paul Revere, Andrew Jackson, Harriet Tubman, Frederick Douglass, Jim Beckwourth, Jim Thorpe, Rosa Parks, and Rachel Carson.

Rookie Biographies (Childrens Press, 1991-1993).
  Individual titles include biographies of Daniel Boone, Robert E. Lee, Martin Luther King, Jr., and Rachel Carson.

We The People Biography Series (Creative Education Publishers, 1988).
  Includes books about Squanto, Francis Marion, Paul Revere, John Paul Jones, Daniel Boone, Dolley Madison, Harriet Tubman, Clara Barton, Kit Carson, Chief Joseph, and Jane Addams.

MAJOR SOURCES USED

The following publications provided a great deal of information in the writing of this book.

The American Heritage History of the Great West; *History of World War II*, both published in 1982.

Dictionary of American Biography, Merriam-Webster, Springfield, MA, 1992.

Eric Foner and John A. Garraty, eds., *The Readers Companion to American History*, Boston: Houghton Mifflin, 1991.

John Grafton, *America: A History of the First 500 Years*, Avinel, NJ: Crescent Books, 1992.

David C. King and others, *The United States and Its People*, Menlo Park: Addison-Wesley, 1993.

Arthur Schlesinger, Jr., ed., *The Almanac of American History*, New York: Barnes & Noble, Inc., 1993.

Bradley Smith, *The USA: A History in Art*, New York: Crowell, 1975.

Webster's American Biographies, Merriam-Webster, Springfield, MA, 1993.

Colonial America

Jamestown National Historic Site, Jamestown Island, Virginia

Includes archaeological findings of the original buildings. Artifacts and replicas of Jamestown are in the Colonial National Historical Park, Yorktown, Virginia.

Plymouth Plantation, Plymouth, Massachusetts

A restoration of Plymouth Plantation.

Cumberland Gap National Historical Park, in southeastern Kentucky, western Virginia, and northern Tennessee

The park includes the Gap and part of the Wilderness road.

The American Revolution

Old North Church and Paul Revere National Historic Landmarks, Boston, Massachusetts

Williamsburg Historic District National Historic Landmark, Williamsburg, Virginia

The many restored buildings include the Raleigh Tavern, where Patrick Henry and other Patriot leaders met.

U.S. Naval Academy National Historic Landmark, Annapolis, Maryland

The museum contains weapons, ship models, flags, and oil paintings. John Paul Jones's crypt is in the Chapel.

The Early United States

Decatur House National Historic Landmark, Washington, D.C.

The White House, Washington, D.C.

The painting of George Washington rescued by Dolley Madison is on display in the East room.

Jean Lafitte National Historic Park and Preserve, New Orleans, Louisiana

The park includes the site of the Battle of New Orleans, with some of the original fortifications.

The Civil War Era

Frederick Douglass Home, Washington, D.C.

General Grant National Memorial, New York, New York

Robert E. Lee Memorial at Arlington National Cemetery, Arlington, Virginia

Arlington also includes of the graves of the Kennedys and of Robert Peary

Appomattox Court House National Historical Park, Appomattox, Virginia

The house in which Robert E. Lee surrendered to Ulysses S. Grant has been rebuilt and includes a museum, with audio-visual presentations.

Heroes of the West

Buffalo Bill Historical Center, Cody, Wyoming
>   Includes exhibits, art, and artifacts related to the movement westward.

Nez Percé National Historical Park, east of Lewiston, Idaho
>   This huge park contains 24 historic sites, including battlefields.

The Early Twentieth Century

Hull House, located at the University of Chicago, Chicago, Illinois
>   The original Hull House has been preserved much as it was when Jane Addams was alive.

The Football Hall of Fame, Canton, Ohio
>   Includes exhibits relating to Jim Thorpe's football career.

Smithsonian Institution, Washington, D.C.
>   Charles A. Lindbergh's *The Spirit of St. Louis* is among the displays.

America Since 1950

Martin Luther King, Jr., Home, Atlanta, Georgia

Civil Rights Memorial, Montgomery, Alabama

John F. Kennedy Space Center, Cape Canaveral, Florida

Rachel Carson Wildlife Refuge, Kennebunkport, Maine

INDEX

Photo Credits